Burton Raffel is professor emeritus at the University of Louisiana at Lafayette and an eminent poet and translator. He is the author of numerous books of literary criticism, including *How to Read a Poem*, and critically acclaimed translations of such works as *Beowulf* and *Don Quixote*.

Brenda Webster has published four novels, including *The Beheading Game* (a finalist for the Northern California Book Reviewers prize) and *Vienna Triangle*, which explores Freud's role in the death of his most brilliant disciple, as well as two oft-anthologized psychoanalytic studies of Yeats and Blake. President of PEN West American Center, she is also the author of a memoir, *The Last Good Freudian*.

Neil D. Isaacs, professor emeritus of English language and literature at the University of Maryland, is the author of numerous books including *Structural Principles of Old English Poetry*.

SIR GAWAIN AND THE GREEN KNIGHT

Translated and with a Preface by
Burton Raffel

A New Introduction by
Brenda Webster

and an Afterword by
Neil D. Isaacs

SIGNET CLASSICS

SIGNET CLASSICS
Published by New American Library, a division of
Penguin Group (USA) Inc., 375 Hudson Street,
New York, New York 10014, USA
Penguin Group (Canada), 90 Eglinton Avenue East, Suite 700, Toronto,
Ontario M4P 2Y3, Canada (a division of Pearson Penguin Canada Inc.)
Penguin Books Ltd., 80 Strand, London WC2R 0RL, England
Penguin Ireland, 25 St. Stephen's Green, Dublin 2,
Ireland (a division of Penguin Books Ltd.)
Penguin Group (Australia), 250 Camberwell Road, Camberwell, Victoria 3124,
Australia (a division of Pearson Australia Group Pty. Ltd.)
Penguin Books India Pvt. Ltd., 11 Community Centre, Panchsheel Park,
New Delhi - 110 017, India
Penguin Group (NZ), 67 Apollo Drive, Rosedale, North Shore 0632,
New Zealand (a division of Pearson New Zealand Ltd.)
Penguin Books (South Africa) (Pty.) Ltd., 24 Sturdee Avenue,
Rosebank, Johannesburg 2196, South Africa

Penguin Books Ltd., Registered Offices:
80 Strand, London WC2R 0RL, England

Published by Signet Classics, an imprint of New American Library, a division
of Penguin Group (USA) Inc. Previously published in a Mentor edition.

First Signet Classics Printing, November 2001
First Signet Classics Printing (Webster Introduction), February 2009
24

For Stefan

CONTENTS

Preface   9

Introduction   43

Sir Gawain and the Green Knight   53

Afterword   135

Selected Bibliography   155

PREFACE

Writers need a very great deal of luck, sometimes, for their work to attract and to hold general attention. All kinds of accidents can and do happen, either to make a writer known, or to prevent him from being known. Geoffrey Chaucer had more luck than most: his South East Midland (London) dialect became the standard form of the language, and Chaucer thereby became "the father of English poetry" (the words are John Dryden's). Chaucer's immediate descendants, though, the so-called Scottish Chaucerians, had the ill luck to write in fifteenth-century Scots—and who outside the universities (and Scotland) today knows the work of Robert Henryson, William Dunbar, or Gavin Douglas? In Scotland, at least, there are extrinsic reasons for studying the older Scots poets. But there are no extrinsic reasons of any great force for studying a fourteenth-century romance, written in some obscure north-country dialect (even the precise nature of the *Gawain*-poet's dialect is still undecipherable), by an unknown poet who may (or may not) have also written three other rather less interesting poems bound into the same manuscript volume. Chaucer is the start of a great tradition; Henryson and Dunbar are part of two traditions, that of English and that of Scots poetry; but the *Gawain*-poet's tradition, though he very probably had one, is unknown to us, and almost certainly unknowable by us, at this distance in time.

Yet *Sir Gawain and the Green Knight* (the title is

not the author's, but has been generally agreed upon since the poem's reappearance, in 1839) is a very great poem, equal to the masterworks of Chaucer or to the best of the old English poems, including *Beowulf.* It is different from these other masterpieces, but it is different from everything else in English literature. The *Gawain*-poet can do an incredible number of things in brilliant style. His sensibility is both delicate and powerful, as is his language; he can sing like a choirboy or like an angry blacksmith; he can draw characters so vividly that they breathe, he can paint pictures so vitally that one sees them, almost feels them. He can weave a compelling and tightly organized plot out of disparate and sometimes fragile elements; he can be passionately moral; he can be wickedly comic (this side of his work has been least well appreciated, to date). Consider the following passage, the decapitation of the green man by Gawain, in King Arthur's court:

Gauan gripped to his ax, and gederes hit on hyȝt,
þe kay fot on þe folde he before sette,
Let hit doun lyȝtly on þe naked,
þat þe scharp of þe schalk schyndered þe bones,
And schrank þurȝ þe schyire grece, and schade hit in twynne,
þat þe bit of þe broun stel bot on þe grounde.
þe fayre hede fro þe halce hit to þe erþe,
þat fele hit foyned wyth her fete, þere hit forth roled;
þe blod brayd fro þe body, þat blykked on þe grene;
And nawþer faltered ne fel þe freke neuer þe helder,
Bot styþly he start forth vpon styf schonkes,
And runyschly he raȝt out, þere as renkkez stoden,
Laȝt to his lufly hed, and lyft hit vp sone;
And syþen boȝez to his blonk, þe brydel he cachchez,
Steppez into stelbawe and strydez alofte,
And his hed by þe here in his honde haldez;
And as sadly þe segge hym in his sadel sette
As non vnhap had hym ayled, þaȝ hedlez he were
in stedde.

He brayde his bulk aboute,
þat vgly bodi þat bledde;
Moni on of hym had doute,
Bi þat his resounz were redde.

Chosen almost at random, this neatly illustrates many
of my claims for the *Gawain*-poet—but who can read
it, today? I decided to translate the poem, though I
do not approve of translating most Middle English
verse, after assigning a section of it, in the original, to
students in a graduate seminar in medieval literature,
students who had already spent more than a full se-
mester reading, also in the original texts, thirteenth-,
fourteenth-, and fifteenth-century lyrics, fourteenth-
and fifteenth-century prose, and verse romances of the
thirteenth and fourteenth centuries. The students were
completely floored. It was a very good class, but
though they worked at *Gawain* with a will they could,
after long hours, just barely decipher it; worse still,
appreciation was paralyzed by the draining effort.

Gawain hefted the axe, swung it high
In both hands, balancing his left foot in front of him,
Then quickly brought it down. The blade
Cut through bones and skin and fair
White flesh, split the green man's neck
So swiftly that its edge slashed the ground.
And the head fell to the earth, rolled
On the floor, and the knights kicked it with their feet:
The body spurted blood, gleaming
Red on green skin—but the green man stood
A moment, not staggering, not falling, then sprang
On strong legs and roughly reached through thrashing
Feet, claimed his lovely head,
And carrying it to his horse caught the bridle,
Stepped in the stirrups and mounted, holding
His head by its long green hair, sitting
High and steady in the saddle as though nothing
Had happened. But he sat there headless, for everyone
                                    To see,

Twisting his bloody, severed
Stump. And the knights were wary,
Afraid before he ever
Opened that mouth to speak.

(Lines 421–443)

Delicacy: the color alternation, first white and green,
then—after the decapitation—red and green; the pre-
cise, balanced care with which details are marshaled.
Power: the forceful evocation of the chopped-off head,
rolling wildly on the floor; the green man, headless,
shoving his way after his head, and claiming it like a
runaway football; his weird, dramatic pose, headless,
bloody, "holding/His head by its long green hair." The
music matches the dominant tone, in each case; the
character of the green man is wonderfully vivid, as are
the characters of the terrified knights of the Round
Table, frantically kicking at the chopped-off head as
it rolls at them. And all the time the story line is
moving forward, while simultaneously there is a subtle
laying down of the elements of the poem's symbolic
morality—as I shall indicate later on. And the comedy:
the chopped-off-head-as-football, but wild and danger-
ous football; the green knight grimacing and making
fierce faces at the knights, by now frightened half out
of their wits; the macabre joke of the green knight
"twisting his bloody, severed/Stump" for "everyone to
see," to make sure that no one misses any of the fun.
It is often black humor; there is also a serious side,
even to the funniest parts—but we know that kind of
thing from Shakespeare. Is there a gorier play than
Hamlet? Is there a funnier play? Each of the elements,
the high drama and the comedy, is in its place, and
each is more effective for its juxtaposition with the
other, heightened, deepened. And the uncertainty is
an integral part of this intensification: you never know,
as mere reader or spectator, whether it will be high
drama or comedy which develops out of a particular
scene. Hamlet rolling in Ophelia's grave, indeed, is a
passionate mixture of both. *Sir Gawain and the Green*

Knight is not *Hamlet,* nor do I want to claim for it that ultimate degree of passion; no truly medieval poet can do the kinds of things Shakespeare does. But *Gawain* is great poetry, it is unqualifiedly a masterpiece. And it needs translation, though Chaucer does not, and even Langland's *Piers Plowman* can be deciphered with a bit of help. Or, to put it a bit differently, it is time that the *Gawain*-poet's luck turned.

There is no information whatever, of any kind whatever, as to who the *Gawain*-poet might have been. A few things are clear, but only a few, from the poem itself. He knew both French and French poetry, and both were important to him: he quite probably lived in (or came from; there is no way of telling) the northwest provinces, but his cultural background was not in the usual sense provincial. He knew a good deal about theology, and cared about his Christianity. He was personally familiar with much of aristocratic life—warfare, armor, hunting, chivalric codes of behavior, protocol—and may well, I suspect, have been himself either an aristocrat, or, I think a little less likely, may have been someone attached to an aristocratic household in a gentlemanly capacity—a tutor, say, or a private secretary.

Everything else is the vaguest speculation, about as idle as the Bacon/Shakespeare or the Earl of Oxford/Shakespeare nonsense. There are no hard facts: the single surviving manuscript is not the author's own copy, and there is no way of knowing how many copies away from the author's own copy it is. The manuscript is a typical scribal job, one of the "publications" of a rural scriptorium—that is, a commercial copying house, which "published" books in the only way then known, by making hand copies. The scribe in this case is neither better nor worse than other commercial practitioners. Some of his mistakes are obvious; some are not obvious, and infuriating; and in all cases the textual scholars have been squabbling, and will continue to squabble, for many years about what the true reading should be. Scholarly editing has produced a generally readable and reliable text, however, and there is substantial agreement even as to the meaning of most difficult passages and words. (Most, but not all, as I shall indicate later.) Incidentally, one slightly unusual feature of the manuscript is its illustrations (unusual because they are not part of the written page, but are done on separate sheets). These illustrations are further indication of the "hack" quality of the provincial scriptorium which produced the book, since they bear very little resemblance to the matter supposed to be illustrated (e.g., the green knight's beard is shown as no longer than Gawain's, and his hair is no longer—and his face and hair are not even green, though green is one of the colors used!).

There is no firm date for the poem, either, nor any solid way of arriving at one. Sometime between, say, 1350 and 1400, is about when the evidence of the handwriting, and other features of the same sort, would seem to indicate. Again, some people are more certain about this than they have any right to be: "The latest possible date is obviously that of the manuscript [true enough], which can hardly be later than 1400 [pure fudge: it is not likely, as far as anyone can now know, to be later than 1400, but there is a lot that no one now knows and much that no one will ever know]; but it is plainly not the author's original and there is no way of telling how often or at what interval it may have been copied." (*Sir Gawain and the Green Knight,* ed. J. R. R. Tolkien and E. V. Gordon, 2nd ed., ed. Norman Davis, Oxford U.P., 1967, p. xxv) There is a slightly strange sense of unreality, to my mind, in even the kind of apparently modest formulation which says, for example, that "the architecture, the costume, the armour, so accurately described, are appropriate to a date between 1360 and 1400." (Laura Hibbard Loomis, as quoted in Marie Borroff, *Sir Gawain and the Green Knight: A Stylistic and Metrical Study,* Yale U.P., 1962, p. 220) They are "appropriate," that is, if it can safely be assumed that the *Gawain*-poet looked out of the window, as it were, and simply described what he himself saw in his own day-to-day existence. Even with the strictly minimal understanding that we have of *Gawain* in its literary context, however, it is clear that there are backward-looking, archaizing elements in both the poem and the culture which produced it. "By 1390 the ideals in . . . *Sir Gawayne* . . . were perhaps consciously old-fashioned. They were even becoming a little insular. . . . It is Chaucer, not the author of *Sir Gawayne,* who could have been appreciated in contemporary Paris." (Gervase Mathew, "Ideals of Knighthood in Late-Fourteen-Century England," in *Twentieth Century Interpretations of Sir Gawain and the Green Knight,* ed. Denton Fox, Prentice-Hall, 1968, p. 72) I do not mean to argue the 1360–1400 date, but only to be suspicious of anything so heavily deductive: that the "appropriate" can in fact be wrong has been shown, recently, even with regard to the much older culture of classical Greece. (See Gerald E. Else, *The Origin and Early Form of Greek Tragedy,* Harvard U.P., 1965, p. 6 n. 8.)

Author, date, dialect: all these are unknown, but we have not done, there is more that is mysterious about the poem. Before the Norman Conquest (1066, and all that), when the English language and English culture generally were much closer to their basic Indo-Germanic roots, poetry had been composed according to a highly developed alliterative prosody. That is, the heavily stressed nature of English, even more obvious in Old than in Modern English, encouraged the *scop* (the only adequate translation is "bard") to work out an organizing principle for poetry which involved a continuous series of matched alliterations.

> *O*ft him *a*nhaga　　*a*re ge*b*ideth,
> *m*etudes *m*iltse,　　þeah þe　　he *m*odcearig . . .

These are the first two lines of the Old English elegy "The Wanderer"; more or less literally, they read: "Often the lonely one prays for mercy,/the grace of God, while sadly he . . ." (In my *Poems From the Old*

English, University of Nebraska Press, 1960, these lines are translated: "This lonely traveler longs for grace,/For the mercy of God; grief hangs on/His heart . . .") The details of this versification, and its relationship to that of *Sir Gawain and the Green Knight,* are discussed in the Afterword. What needs to be said, here, is that Old English prosody disappears, or seems to disappear, with the Norman Conquest. When poetry reappears in the later form of the language which we call Middle English, the prosody is obviously very different. The first poem in Carleton Brown's *English Lyrics of the XIIIth Century,* Oxford U.P., 1932, reads:

> Nou goth sonne vnder wod,—
> me reweth, marie, þi faire Rode.
> Nou goþ sonne vnder tre,—
> me reweþ, marie, þi sone and þe.

> Now goes the sun under the forest (wood),
> I mourn, Mary, your beautiful face.
> Now goes the sun under the tree,
> I mourn, Mary, thy son and thee.

Probably written in 1239, this little lyric is an iambic tetrameter rhyming quatrain, with an A A B B rhyme scheme. The alliteration of *r*eweth and *R*ode, in line 2, is ornamental, rather than structural. And this kind of prosody, these kinds of poetic forms, are plainly what we recognize as English prosody, English poetic forms, from Chaucer to Yeats. This is the prosody of Spenser, of Shakespeare, of Donne, of Milton, Dryden, Pope, Wordsworth, Keats—of virtually everyone before World War I, and of many poets still writing today.

But it is not the prosody, or the poetic form, used by the *Gawain*-poet. He is clearly aware of the newer prosody; this is plain from the so-called "bob-and-wheel," the five-line rhymed tag at the end of each strophe of *Sir Gawain:*

> . . . in stedde.
> He brayde his bulk aboute,
> þat vgly bodi þat bledde;
> Moni on of hym had doute,
> Bi þat his resounz were redde.

Even in the bob-and-wheel, however, alliteration is too strong, too basic really, to be simply ornamental: *b*rayde/*b*ulk/a*b*oute is followed by *b*odi/*b*ledde, and in the last line by *r*esounz/*r*edde. And in the main part of each strophe (I use "strophe" rather than "stanza," since the length varies from as few as 12 lines to as many as 37, and since the poet seems to feel free to vary the length as he pleases) it is very definitely alliteration that makes the line work, that holds it together:

> *G*auan gripped to his ax, and *g*ederes hit on hy*ȝ*t,
> þe kay *f*ot on þe *f*olde he be*f*ore *s*ette . . .

Gawain is not at all an isolated example of Middle English alliterative verse. *Piers Plowman,* too, works on an alliterative rather than a meter-and-rhyme pattern:

> In a *s*omere *s*eyson, whan *s*ofte was the *s*onne,
> Y *sh*op me into *sh*robbis, as y a *sh*epherde *w*ere,
> In *a*bit as an *e*rmite, vn*h*oly of *w*erkes . . .

(In Henry W. Wells' translation, *The Vision of Piers Plowman,* Sheed and Ward, 1935, "In a summer season when the sun was softest/Shrouded in a smock, in a shepherd's clothing,/In the habit of a hermit of unholy living . . .") This is neither the same dialect nor exactly the same alliterative prosody as that of *Gawain* (again, this is something which is discussed in the Afterword). What is remarkable is that at least two extraordinarily fine poets, and a great many lesser ones (some of whose work has survived, though it is not always worth reading), were writing in a style thought to have been dead for almost three centuries. (Laȝamon's *Brut,* written about 1200, is much closer to the Old English, in metric, language, and spirit.) Mischristened "the alliterative revival," this renaissance of a prosodic phoenix *cannot* really be a "revival." Old English prosody plainly did not die, but rather went underground, to surface once more, as the English language itself finally surfaced, after its long domination by Norman French, in the fourteenth century. Consider how Chaucer separates "northern" men from "southern" men; southerners write as he himself writes, but northerners write in the strange, provincial, faintly ludicrous alliterative mode:

> But trusteth wel, I am a Southren man,
> I kan nat geeste "rum, ram, ruf," by lettre,
> Ne, Got woot, rym holde I but litel bettre.

("Geeste" means to tell a tale; the passage occurs in the Parson's Prologue, lines 42–44.) This kind of easy familiarity with a northern, alliterative style seems to me almost conclusive evidence—and notice, too, that "rum, ram, ruf" is explicitly juxtaposed against "rym." And consider the following passage from that still much misunderstood story, "The Knight's Tale." In part four of the poem, as the tournament is ready to begin, Chaucer makes cheerful, subtle fun of the institution of knighthood, not directly, but by making fun of alliterative poetry. In his mind, and in his audience's, alliterative prosody is automatically associated with moribund, anachronistic chivalric values and customs:

> . . . In gooth the *sh*arpe *s*pore into the *s*yde.
> Ther seen men who kan juste and who kan ryde;
> Ther *sh*yveren *sh*aftes upon *sh*eeldes thikke;
> He feeleth thurgh the herte-spoon the prikke.
> Up *s*pryngen *sp*eres twenty foot on highte;
> Out goon the *s*werdes as the *s*ilver brighte;
> The *h*elmes they to*h*ewen and toshrede;

Out *b*rest the *b*lood with *st*ierne *st*remes rede;
With *m*yghty *m*aces the *b*ones they to*b*reste.
He *th*urgh the *th*ikkeste of the *th*rong gan *th*reste;
Ther *st*omblen *st*eedes *st*ronge, and doun gooth al;
He *f*oyneth on his *f*eet with his *t*ronchoun,
And *h*e hym *h*urtleth with his *h*ors adoun . . .
(Fragment I, lines 2603–2616)

Whatever the full significance of this, in "The Knight's Tale" itself, I think it shows that Chaucer has not only heard of alliterative verse, but has heard (or read) the thing itself. And, further, he expects his (London) audience to have the same kind of familiarity. That kind of generally shared, easy knowledge does not fit, I think, with a moribund metric sprung suddenly to life. As Roger Sherman Loomis puts it, "the Alliterative Revival . . . might be termed more accurately the Alliterative Survival." (*The Development of Arthurian Romance,* Harper Torchbooks, 1964, p. 147)

There is no way of taking this much further, still: not enough is (or may ever be) known about the culture from which *Gawain* emerged, and in which the *Gawain*-poet was nurtured. But the difficulty caused by the "missing link" does not prevent anthropologists from noting the difference between Pithecanthropus and the gorilla. ("Do not try to make an ape out of Pithecanthropus," says William Howells, "or Pithecanthropus may make a monkey out of you." *Mankind So Far,* Doubleday, 1945, p. 137)

The *Gawain*-poet writes, sometimes, the way late-medieval artists paint, or tapestry-makers weave.

With the New Year drawing close, courtiers
And ladies sat to a double feast;
Mass had been sung in the chapel, the king
And his knights came to the hall, and priests
And laymen called "Noël! Noël!"
And shouted and sang, and nobles ran

> With New Year's presents in their hands, noisily
> Passing in a crowd, calling "Presents!
> Presents!" and loudly disputing gifts,
> While ladies laughed when kisses were lost
> (And whoever won them found it hard to weep),
> And till dinnertime came they ran and laughed . . .
> *(Lines 60–71)*

There is a sense of great vitality, a feeling of enthusiastic motion, but always dominated by the poet's translucent way of seeing. This passage is not cinematic, in our twentieth-century sense, though it throngs with motion and the voices and the laughter are distinctly audible. It is not cinematic because the principle of subordination, the trick of seeing things only in linear perspective, is not usual to the late-medieval sensibility. It is like the Duc de Berry's *Book of Hours*: the foreground is rich, vital, but though the background is clearly the background, though the basic laws of perspective are usually taken into account, the background is not simply background, is not in that sense subordinated. The painters of Renaissance Italy, when they opened a window behind a portrait figure, and showed a winding road up a hill, and little trees and houses fading into the distance, were in fact subordinating; their background is impossible to confuse with their foreground. In the Duc de Berry's *Book of Hours* there is neither confusion nor equivalence, but rather a kind of simultaneity, a kind of nonlinear perception of two—or more—worlds at the same time. For beyond the background, there is usually another background, usually architectural rather than human— and beyond that second background there is a third, the decorative astrological work enscrolled across the top of the page. There is something very like this in the passage from *Gawain*: we see the courtiers and their ladies, who are the foreground, but the priests are there too, and the laymen are there too, and when the nobles run through the crowd, shouting "Presents! Presents!" the crowd is somehow particularized too.

The twentieth-century camera can see only the perspective, can see only the subordination, only the motion through time or through space. For the camera to see, to fix, a whole scene, the camera must stop (as it does, with marvelous poignancy, at the end of *Elvira Madigan*: that frozen moment in time, which one knows is not actually frozen, powerfully evokes what the passage of time has brought, and what it has destroyed). But the *Gawain*-poet sees both the perspective and the stasis, the motion and the imperishable, fixed things.

> The horses ran, when they could, on the gravel
> Path. Morning slid past and was gone.
> The whole brave company came riding to Herot,
> Anxious to celebrate Beowulf's success . . .
> > (Beowulf, *lines 916–919; my translation,*
> > *New American Library, 1963)*

Apart from the differences of tone and general style, which are large differences, the difference between this little scene from *Beowulf,* and the similarly festive scene from *Gawain,* seems to me in some senses the difference between the abstract and the particular. The *Beowulf-scop* is interested in qualities, states; the movements he sees are large ones, even group ones. Even in deadly hand-to-hand combat, Beowulf seems less an embattled *man* than a struggling will, fighting hard against another equally determined but less powerfully focused will. Beowulf needs only to be in full focus—"Holy/God, who sent him victory, gave judgment/For truth and right, Ruler of the Heavens,/Once Beowulf was back on his feet and fighting" (lines 1553–1556)—and the battle is as good as over. In the sense for which battle is battle, for the *Gawain*-poet, battle is not battle, in *Beowulf.* It is, as I said before, something much more abstract, something no less real but a great deal less particular.

And the *Gawain*-poet's visual particularity is usually

even more tapestry-like than my first example. Consider this:

> A beard
> As thick as a bramble-bush grew from his chin
> And fell in front as far as the hair
> In back, hair and beard cut
> At the elbow, like a king's hooded cape
> Enclosing his neck and half his arms;
> And his horse's mane hung long, combed
> And curled, braided strand for strand
> With gold thread, a strand of green hair,
> Another of gold; and his forelock, and his tail
> Were braided to match, bound in place
> With a green band, dotted with precious
> Stones the length of that flowing tail,
> Then laced with an elaborate knot, and strung
> With dozens of bright gold bells that rang
> As he rode . . .
>
> *(Lines 181–196)*

This is incomparably visual. Perhaps the most impressive thing I can say about it—and I am talking from experience, not from theory—is that it can give to a twentieth-century sensibility, oriented to visual images, a satisfaction very like that given by, say, the vivid miniatures of the Duc de Berry's *Book of Hours*. (I mean that part of the *Book of Hours* which was executed in 1413–1416. The rest of the work, completed in the 1480s by a different artist, is still very beautiful, but is much less particular; in the intervening more than half a century, the medieval esthetic had faded very fast, in all art forms.) The poem is full of brightly colored miniatures, more in the first half than the second—but see, for example, the extraordinary scene of lines 1694–1697, or the intense weather picture of lines 2000–2005:

> The world was beautiful, hung with frost,
> And the huge red sun rose through clouds

And came, white and gleaming, to the sky.
Beside a wood they unleashed their hounds . . .

   . . . But storms crackled through the world,
Clouds tumbled their bitter cold
On the earth, northwinds freezing the poor;
Snow shivered in the air, and animals
Shook; the wind whistled from the hills
And drove snowdrifts down in the valleys. . . .

Even in the second half of the poem, when the scenes
have been set and the story line, quite naturally, tends
to dominate, the poet's need to *see,* his intensely visual
sensibility, is unmistakable.

I have said a good deal about the *Gawain*-poet's
technique and about his late-medieval sensibility. I
have said very little, still, about his poem—and the
delay is not accidental. *Sir Gawain and the Green
Knight* is a complex and a brilliant poem, but it is
especially complex and brilliant on the surface; it has
as much *interior* as any other great poem, but it has
rather more *exterior.* It cannot be approached, there-
fore, by focusing on its meaning—not even to the de-
gree that such an approach can be valid for poems
like *Beowulf,* say, or *The Poem of the Cid,* or *La
Chanson de Roland.* It is neither possible nor is it
sensible to try to say, simply and directly, what *Sir
Gawain* is about. Larry D. Benson, whose *Art and
Tradition in Sir Gawain and the Green Knight* (Rut-
gers U.P., 1965) is far and away the best book on the
poem, shows this very neatly, in discussing the green-
ness of the green knight: "The green skin is puzzling
because that is what the poet intended it to be." (p.
91) Benson goes on: "It is the ambiguity of the green-
ness and the relevance of its ambiguous implications
to the challenger's character that maintain the balance
of attractiveness and fearfulness . . ." (p. 92) The key
words are "ambiguity" and "balance." The *Gawain*-
poet, as I suggested earlier, is interested in portraying

a kind of simultaneity, a kind of nonlinear perception of two—or more—worlds at the same time. Benson is worth citing at some length, on this:

> This final scene is only an extension of the recurrent alternation of romance and unromantic elements that repeatedly undercuts the high seriousness of the narrative. . . . The Green Knight . . . has an attitude of his own, unromantic rather than anti-romantic in its refusal to take romance seriously. . . . The poem is thus both a tragic romance with the sad moral that perfection is beyond our grasp and an unromantic comedy with the happy point that if a man aims high enough he can come as near perfection as this world allows.
>
> *(pp. 242, 243)*

And Benson shows, to my mind, a singularly sure touch when he observes, in his final paragraph, that "whatever deeper concerns it has touched and however serious it almost becomes, *Sir Gawain* is predominantly a festive poem." (p. 248)

One of the chief things that the poem is about, one of the *Gawain*-poet's central concerns, is knighthood. The fact that he knows as much about it as he does, and can marshal his expert's knowledge with an easy concision, is one kind of proof that he takes knighthood seriously. He would not bother with the details of armor (in fact he obviously takes an almost nostalgic relish in them), and in what order each carefully described and labeled part is put on, and just how it is put on, if his concern was not fundamentally serious. But neither is he uncritical. I have already indicated that he rather makes fun of the knights of the Round Table. It's almost worse than that: he shows the knights as courtly, highly verbal, socially accomplished men who neither enjoy nor in fact often engage in knightly combat. He shows the great King Arthur "boisterous and merry as a boy . . . His blood ran young, and his brain was restless." (Lines 85, 87) Even his hero, "Gawain the good," fights his real battles in bed—which had become pretty much Gawain's contemporary reputation. ("To sum up: in the romances, prose as well as verse, Gawain is the casual, good-natured and well-mannered wooer of almost any available girl. . . . Gawain as a lover followed a well-defined pattern: when he met an unattached girl he made love to her; if she rebuffed him he departed; if, as more often, she welcomed his attentions, he also departed, but not as soon." B. J. Whiting, "Gawain: His Reputation, His Courtesy, and His Appearance in Chaucer's *Squire's Tale*," in Denton Fox, *op. cit.* pp. 74, 75. The knight-rapist of "The Wife of Bath's Tale," incidentally, is in many other versions of the same story identified as Sir Gawain.) Gawain is brave, and he is chivalric, and as the *Gawain*-poet portrays him he is essentially moral, but the very plethora of talk about his immense knightly reputation serves to undercut, in fact, our belief in the reality of that reputation.

What Gawain *does*, really, is something much more like what a Christian martyr might be expected to do, rather than a typical knightly performance. He swings one initial axe stroke, at a passive target; except for the hastily dismissed combats with dragons, satyrs, trolls, and the like (all crammed into lines 716–725), all of them met with by the way, on his way to the green chapel, Gawain never fights again. What he does have to do is wait for and think about death, and struggle with earthly temptations. Nor does he overcome those temptations: the resemblance to a martyr ceases, at this point. Gawain manages, but just barely, to keep from making love to his host's beautiful and all-too-willing wife; he preserves a kind of formal chastity, though he looks rather bedraggled about it, by the third day of the beautiful lady's seductive vamping. But he does not manage to keep from cheating, to keep from—in his terms—treachery and betrayal, when the lady offers him a magic belt, capable (she says) of preserving his life when he will finally bow his head to the green man's axe. He succumbs quite expeditiously, and knows it: when the host returns from his day's hunting, on that third day, there is no need to seek Gawain out, as there has been before. Gawain is waiting, eager to pass on the kisses the host's wife gave him that morning—but equally eager not to pass on the belt. More: Gawain practically rushes from the scene of his fall (his bed) to make confession—after hiding the magic belt "in a safe place,/Covering it carefully so he could find it later." (Lines 1874–1875) There has been a certain amount of loose talk about this confession: did Gawain confess about the belt, or didn't he? Was the absolution valid, or was it *ab initio* invalid? And there has been the usual wearisome parade of ecclesiastical learning, none of it relevant—for the elementary truth would seem to be that Gawain confesses because he has an overwhelming need to, because he has an overwhelming—and quite justified—sense of guilt and sin. He of course does not tell the confessing priest about the belt: he might otherwise be instructed to return it to the lady, or to admit to his host that he has accepted it and be obliged to pass it back, along with the lady's kisses, as part of his exchange-of-winnings bargain—and hadn't he and the lady, to whom he was obliged, as knight and as man, "agreed that only/She and Gawain would share the secret/Forever"? (Lines 1863–1865) But he finds relief in confessing and being told that "his soul/Was anointed so completely clean that the Day/Of Judgment could have come with the sun, and been welcome." (Lines 1882–1884) It does not matter that this is not "true": truth is how one feels it, as the *Gawain*-poet knows and too many of his critics do not—and on the level for which Gawain needed this absolution it is true and valid and a relief, it is everything he expected it would be. He does not want to die: that is primary. If he has already cheated on the basic code of his professional, knightly existence, as he clearly has, what does it matter that in a sense he has now cheated on God? And indeed is there any difference? Integrity is integrity: once it is forfeited, it is forfeited. Period. The proof of the pudding, I think, is that after his confession Gawain is uproariously happy; the poet goes far out of his way, taking eight full lines for the description, to report that his hero was now "making merry/As never before in that house" (Lines 1886–1887), and that all the host's men noticed and were delighted at their guest's flowing joy. Gawain has been politely merry, before this; he has drunk the wine and told the jokes—but now for the first time his heart is in it. Having fallen, at last, he is happy: "Now leave him in that comfort, *where love had come to him!*" (Line 1893; my italics), the poet assures us, as he turns from Gawain to the host (and it is the traditionally deceitful fox that the host is hunting). "Comfort," yes, but "where *love* had come to him"? The poet knows perfectly well that it was not love but the safety of his neck that had come to Gawain: the line is blatantly ironic, and so serves further to undercut the hero's moral standing.

Which is on yet another level what the poem is about—only on one level, since as I said this is not a poem capable of being analyzed on any but a multitude of levels, all at the same time. "Gawain, in a reversal of the pattern of romances like *Caradoc* and *Perceval,* starts as a perfect knight and moves downward, ending where the heroes of those romances began, as an imperfect 'fol chevalier' who is the object of laughter rather than admiration." (Benson, *op. cit.* p. 242) When the chastened, repentant, super-Christian Gawain returns to King Arthur's court, groaning and moaning about his sinfulness, and proclaiming that the belt is "the mark of my sin" and that he therefore will wear it as long as he lives, he concludes with what seems almost Old English gnomic wisdom: "For a man may hide an injury to his soul,/But he'll never be rid of it, it's fastened forever." (Lines 2511–2512) One can almost begin to believe in Gawain's virtue and repentance, uncritically—but then the king and the whole court pat him on the back, and laugh, and say they'll *all* wear belts of repentance. And they do. And so much for Gawain taking himself quite so seriously, or our doing so either.

Gawain is by no means an anti-hero. When the green knight watches him spouting and waving his sword, after the test is over, "he liked what he saw." (Line 2335) Gawain is brave and eager and alert—and yet, at the same time, he's making an awful fool of himself. The frantic motions he makes, his tumbling, half-stuttering words of warning, are deftly contrasted with the peaceful dignity of the green man, unperturbed, leaning on his great axe and watching, listening. And yet the green man, too, has no morally absolute ground to stand on. He comes as the emissary of a practitioner of black magic, the witch Morgana le Fay; *his* head is never in danger, because of the guarantees of that magic; and his mission is not a terribly noble one, as he himself describes it, being partly designed to test the virtue of the knights of the Round Table, partly designed to frighten Guenevere out of her wits (because of an ancient jealousy between the queen and Morgana). The green knight can be courtly, chivalric, dignified; he can also be rude, boastful, and exceedingly melodramatic. He partakes, in short, of the delicate, deliberate ambiguity of the whole poem. He is partly human, partly force of nature; he is partly moral, partly amoral. (Benson's analysis, *op. cit.* pp. 56 ff., is both brilliantly perceptive and full of learning usefully applied.) Like Gawain, he can speak with dignity and with Right on his side; but also like Gawain, he can seem, whether as green man or as host, considerably less than an ideal symbol of Truth and Goodness. Indeed, those moralizing capital letters seem distinctly out of place anywhere in this poem; it and its poet are far too subtle, too human in the most civilized sense, to indulge in such lack of balance.

I do not mean that the *Gawain*-poet was not a believing Christian, or that his poem is not basically a Christian poem. He was and it is. The description of the pentangle star on Gawain's shield (Lines 619 ff.)

shows a passionate Christianity, and as I have already said Gawain's actions as a knight, and the whole testing tale which underlies the plot of the poem, have a deeply Christian framework. But the poet keeps things always in balance: if he tells us, in the pentangle passage, that Gawain enjoys "freedom from sin" (Line 652), it is necessary to look back to the observation, in the same long passage, that Gawain is "as good as any knight in any gleaming/Castle/And worthy of that star." (Lines 634–636) That is, Gawain is human, not either mythical or saintly; his "freedom from sin" is therefore to be understood as relative, just like everything else in the poem. Gawain prays to Mary, on his journey in search of the green chapel, and after he has three times "shaped the sign of the cross/And called Christ in his need" (Lines 761–762), he is granted the vision of the host's castle, "the loveliest ever owned," and he is joyful, and thankful "for the answering of his prayer." But the castle is also the scene of his destined temptation, and of his destined fall. If such a possibility could be imagined, Gawain would clearly have been better off sleeping in ditches than luxuriating in the host's white sheets, with or without the host's white-skinned wife. The *Gawain*-poet plainly knows this, and just as plainly knows that his almost Hegel-like perception of the antithesis concealed within the synthesis is the only sane way to see things. And he is phenomenally sane.

He is, in fact, so powerful a literary mind that what could be a mere matter of philosophy, with a lesser writer, is transformed for him into a vital matter of literary technique. The balance I have spoken of is a structural device, in *Sir Gawain*. The most famous, and most widely commented-on example, is the alternation of the host's hunting and Gawain's being hunted. There is no need to press relentlessly, as some commentators have done, for exact resemblances between each of the animals being hunted by the host, and the particular nature, day by day, of Gawain's temptations. That kind of dogged parallel-hunting

makes about as much sense as measuring the host's
weapons against Gawain's words, or the host's horse
against Gawain's—but this kind of thing is absurd on
its face. But the structural balancing is very clear. On
the lady's first visit to Gawain, the first day, the scene
starts with a brief recoup of the host's deer-hunting—
"So the lord plays at the edge of the wood"—and
then immediately moves to Gawain, who "lies in a
lovely bed." (Lines 1178, 1179) Fourteen lines further
on, we are told that the lady tiptoed into Gawain's
room, came to where he seems to be sleeping, "and
gently/Sat at the edge of the bed . . ." (Lines 1192–
1193). Her husband hunts at the edge of a wood, she
at the edge of a bed: the parallel is too plain for com-
ment. On the second day, while the boar is being bom-
barded with arrows and bothered, but not hurt by
them, the scene shifts back to Gawain being bom-
barded by the lady: "And so she tested him, pushed
and probed,/Trying to tempt him . . ." (Lines 1549–
1550) The clearest parallel, already noted, is between
the "thieving" fox hunted on the third day by the
husband, and the treacherous Gawain hunted—and
caught—by the wife. The host has brought in noble
game, before, game with rich supplies of meat, to show
for the chase; this time he brings only honor to ex-
change with Gawain—for the fox's tail is distinctly an
honorific rather than an edible trophy. And to match
honor, Gawain brings, for the first time, dishonor. And
yet not absolute dishonor: the green knight himself
tells him, after the trial, that he is still "a pearl/To a
pea, compared to other knights." Gawain fell, but
"Not for a beautiful belt, or in lust,/But for love of
your life. I can hardly blame you." (Lines 2364–2365,
2367–2368) It is all in balance; now that he has fallen,
indeed, Gawain can make a real confession—not to a
priest, but to the force of nature that the green man
here represents.

> "Oh knight: I humbly confess
> My faults: bless me

With the chance to atone.
I'll try to sin less."

(Lines 2385–2388)

I have hardly mentioned what seems to me the most triumphant aspect of the *Gawain*-poet's ripe, civilized balance, namely his wit. It pervades the entire poem, light, dry, and plainly related to things French. Even when the poet uses something like the Old English *litotes* (ironic statements suggesting the opposite of what their words seem to say), he handles it very very differently: when the ladies of Arthur's court are pursued, and caught, and kissed, they laugh at the kisses they've "lost/(And whoever won them found it hard to weep) . . ." (Lines 69–70) More usually, the poet's wit runs like this delicately barbed comment on Arthur: "So the fearless king stood in front of his table,/ Talking of elegant trifles." (Lines 107–108) Arthur is fearless, he does stand, he does chat blandly: the point, the barb, lies in the sly mixture of opposites, the brave king standing not in battle but at his dinner table, and talking not of high morality and courage but of sophisticated nothings. When the knights of the Round Table are flabbergasted by the green knight, "And were afraid to answer him, then gasped at his voice/And trembled, sitting motionless in that noble/ Hall, silent as stones, as corpses . . ." (Lines 241–243), the poet slyly explains the silence as perhaps an act, in part, of "courtesy, to do honor/To Arthur, whose words should come first." (Lines 248–249) This has been taken with deadly seriousness: the poet, says Albert B. Friedman, "attributes the court's speechless fright to their absorption in the appearance of the monster; furthermore he excuses the knights' silence by saying it was not entirely fear that kept them silent but politeness somewhat: protocol demanded that only the king answer." ("Morgan le Fay in *Sir Gawain and the Green Knight*," in Robert J. Blanch, ed., *Sir Gawain and Pearl: Critical Essays*, Indiana U.P., 1966, p. 137) Nonsense: as the green knight cruelly tells

them, "you sit there shaking—at words!" (Line 315)
The significant thing, the morally and the dramatically
significant thing, is that the knights *are* afraid, and
knights are not supposed to feel fear. Arthur, as king,
and Gawain, as the hero of the poem, rise above
their fear: "No one's afraid of your nonsense" (Line
325), Arthur snaps, but I hope no one is taken in
by that kind of disclaimer. Not only are the knights
described as scared witless, not only are they de-
scribed as kicking in panic, when the green man's
decapitated head rolls near them, but even in Part
Two of the poem we are told that "the men/Of the
Round Table sat silent at their meat, stuffed,/Now,
with grim business." (Lines 492–494) The two who
rise above fear have a different reaction: "Arthur and
Gawain grinned/At the joke, and laughed at the
green man." (Lines 463–464) But Arthur and Gawain
are immediately distinguished from everyone else at
the court, and on the basis of all the evidence in the
poem, quite properly distinguished: ". . . those who
had seen him/Knew miracles had been sent." (Lines
465–466)

My favorite among the *Gawain*-poet's barbed pas-
sages is one in which Gawain is permitted to turn the
weapon of wit on his tormentor. The green knight has
begun to swing his axe, Gawain has flinched, and now
the green man is toying with him. "You talk too long,"
Gawain replies, "Perhaps you've frightened yourself
with these threats?" (Lines 2300–2301) There is some-
thing quite magnificent about the frightened, yet now
controlled hero, finally the master of his fear, taunting
his taunter. And the green man, who knows courage
when he sees it, immediately stops clowning and, in
fact, gets it over with. I suppose my next favorite is
the scene in which Gawain suddenly hears the loud,
menacing roar of the huge grindstone which is prepar-
ing an axe for his neck—but there really is no end to
a list of favorite witty passages, in a poem sometimes
so frothy that there have been critics who called it "a
comic poem—by which I mean not so much a poem

full of fun and games (though it is that), as a poem which ends happily . . ." (J. A. Burrow, *A Reading of Sir Gawain and the Green Knight,* Routledge & Kegan Paul, 1965, p. 185) There is a kind of gruesome fascination in setting against this fairly basic perception the so-called critical intelligence which declares that the *Gawain*-poet "is as civilized as Chaucer, but sterner, much more of a moralist, a great deal less of a humorist. But there is humor of a sort in his presentation of the Green Knight's play-acting in Arthur's hall, and in some of Gawain's rueful remarks . . ." (Dorothy Everett, "The Alliterative Revival," in Denton Fox, *op. cit.* p. 22) The same critic—and I shall return to the *Gawain*-critics as a group, shortly—has just before this whopper referred, incredibly, to "the *blustering* words of Gawain as he hears the Green Knight whetting his axe behind the rock." (*Ibid.* at p. 21; my italics) *Blustering?* " 'That's meant for me,' said Gawain,/ 'A kind of greeting. By Christ, I'll greet him/Better./ God's will be done!' . . ." (Lines 2205–2208) *Blustering?* As the *Gawain*-poet's chronological contemporary, Chaucer, put it, at the end of *Troilus and Criseyde*: "Go, litel bok, go, . . . prey I God that non myswrite the,/Ne the mysmetre for defaute of tonge./ And red wherso thow be, or elles songe,/That thow be understonde, God I biseche!" (Book V, lines 1786, 1795–1798)

I have used the Tolkien and Gordon text of the poem *(op. cit.),* as reedited in 1967 by Norman Davis. I have felt perfectly free, however, to disagree with the editors, with or without contrary authorities in hand. (Benson, *op. cit.,* where he has commented on difficult words and phrases, is a superior lexical as well as a critical guide; Marie Borroff's *Sir Gawain and the Green Knight: A Stylistic and Metrical Study, op. cit.,* though because of its announced concerns it should be a still better help with disputed words and phrases, is often deplorably insensitive.) The strange positions which the editors often assume, in both literary and technical matters, do not inspire overwhelming confidence. In discussing line 1284, e.g., they say: "If line 1284 were taken, as it sometimes is, as part of the lady's thought, it would imply that she knew that Gawain was obliged to face the blow from the Green Knight. The story *as presented* has given her no opportunity to know this, so that it would be a serious flaw in the handling of the plot." (p. 110; my italics) But the poet has just finished telling us, three lines earlier, that "Till the middle of the morning they spoke of many/Things, the lady *pretending* to love him . . ." (Lines 1280–1281; italics added) The editors are concerned lest they "spoil the suspense"; I would have them, myself, more concerned with not spoiling the poem. Similarly, when the host's wife ogles and tempts Gawain, and the knight is both tempted and wary, the editors say of the expression *with hymseluen,* in line 1660, that it "must mean 'within himself, in his mind,' not 'angry *at* himself'—for which he had no cause." (p. 118) I translate "angry with himself," here; it seems to me plain that Gawain already has more than enough cause to be annoyed at his own performance. And as I suggested, the editors are more than fallible, even in technical matters where, presumably, their grip should be firmest. They say—the one example will be enough, I think—that "a striking feature of the bob in *Gawain* is that it seldom adds anything essential to the meaning, and is often distinctly redundant . . . It is possible that this element of the stanza was an afterthought of the author's, and that the bobs were added after the poem was complete, with a few adjustments." (p. 152) The bob—that is, the one- or two-word line which immediately precedes the four-line "wheel," and the main function of which is (a) to break the rhythm, and (b) to set the rhyme word for the wheel—is after all a line of one or two words; only once in the poem does it have as many as three words. To ask high drama of it is asking rather a lot, especially considering its important rhyme and rhythmical functions (the latter quite neglected, and perhaps unperceived). But even apart from the bob's brevity, it is simply not true that it "seldom adds anything essential to the meaning": the weasel word is plainly "essential." Note: in line 245, the poet tells us in the bob that Arthur's knights were silent *in hyȝe,* "suddenly"; the bob of line 274 informs us that the green man asks his sport *(gomen) bi ryȝt,* "as a matter of right, as a privilege of the Christmas season"; and in line 338 the bob tells us that the green man ignores Arthur's war-like preparations as he would ignore a manservant bringing him a drink *of wyne.* The examples could be multiplied tenfold, and they point clearly to the fact that the editors have concentrated much more on the arcane trade of *editing* than they have on the much simpler and more direct occupation of understanding, of reading the poem as the poet tried to have us read it. I do not mean to be ungrateful, or to bite the hand that feeds me, but I'm afraid that John Speirs is (for a change) right when he groans that the Tolkien/Gordon/Davis text "merely slavishly reproduces the deficiencies, confusions and inconsistencies of the copyist's spelling in the Cotton Nero IX manuscript." He is right, too, when he attacks the book's "lengthy, mostly irrelevant notes." ("Sir Gawain and the Green Knight," in Denton Fox, *op. cit.* p. 79) Especially in its new paperback incarnation, however, this is the edition most likely to be used by students all across the world, and it is handy and cheap and, as far as it goes, generally reliable.

It is no defense of Tolkien, Gordon, and Davis, but most literary criticism of medieval poetry suffers from just their kind of "lengthy, mostly irrelevant" insensitivity to a poem as a poem. I have referred, several times, to Denton Fox's handy, brief compilation of *Gawain* criticism. It *is* handy, and it is sometimes helpful, though the editor's generally sensible introduction observes, early on, that "The facts about the Middle English alliterative tradition are well known, if somewhat baffling"! (p. 2) But the critics' attention-span is somehow limited by their scholarship, or alternatively

by their desire to assert some interpretive claim. I
have already referred to Dorothy Everett's essay,
"The Alliterative Revival"; it is not all as bad as the
passages I have cited. Nor is Donald R. Howard's
"Structure and Symmetry in *Sir Gawain*," though he
is capable of saying that "the lord's [host's] replies on
receiving the kisses are richly ambiguous, for it is
never wholly clear whether or not he knows what his
wife has been up to." (p. 54) But as the green knight
later tells Gawain, "I know it all, knight,/The kisses
you took, and gave, and all/You did, and how she
tempted you . . ." (Lines 2359–2361) One must be
wary of critics whose minds stray so easily from liter-
ary fact.

And there is even more need to be wary of the
critics in the longer, but much more offensive Blanch
compilation *(op. cit.)*. Albert B. Friedman, referred to
earlier, can write: "To imply that our poet, for all his
moral earnestness, could find anything foolish in the
casual challenges and joustings, which are among the
chief happenings in romances, is to foist upon him an
Ariosto-like attitude that would have disqualified him
from writing this poem." (pp. 137–138) But as Denton
Fox notes, "A hero whose only martial exploit of any
importance is to chop off a proffered head at the be-
ginning of the poem, and whose only amorous exploit
is to refuse a lady's offer of love, is in startling contrast
to the typical hero of a Middle English romance . . .
a glorious, and slightly ridiculous, hero." *(Op. cit.* pp.
5, 12) Was Chaucer "disqualified from writing" *Troi-
lus and Criseyde*—whatever that might mean—because
he explicitly mocks "the casual challenges and joust-
ings, which are among the chief happenings in ro-
mances," in his "The Knight's Tale"? Similarly, Mr.
Friedman can say, soberly, that the host's wife *"forces
Gawain to accept"* the belt, and that "Gawain accepts
it only because of its alleged magical properties *and
to be quit of the nagging importunities of his hostess."*
(p. 145; my italics) I can only gape: where has the
man been?

Alan M. Markman's "The Meaning of *Sir Gawain and the Green Knight*," which follows the Friedman essay, asserts that "the primary purpose of the poem is to show what a splendid man Gawain is." (p. 161) In the light of the poem itself, this is obviously a wonderful conclusion indeed, but since Mr. Markman frequently rewrites the poem, it becomes a dangerous conclusion for an unsuspecting student. Gawain, says Mr. Markman, is "the ideal feudal Christian knight . . . In the very first place we should notice [his] physical fitness for knighthood. Throughout the feudal age the armored cavalryman had to possess strength and endurance," etc., etc. (p. 162) "His agility in placing himself in position to attack after the Green Knight had lightly wounded him on the neck . . . demonstrates the skill at arms which the feudal age demanded of the knight" (p. 163) And the fact that the poet is making fun of Gawain, very jolly fun indeed, in this exact passage? Gone, all gone, as if it had never been.

Richard Hamilton Green follows Mr. Markman's lumpy pages with "Gawain's Shield and the Quest for Perfection." One expects, at once, a high-toned reading of the poem, with liberal shovelings-in of iconographic learning, and Mr. Green delivers as expected. *Sir Gawain* presents us with "an ideal society in a marvelous world where the virtuous hero represents the temporal and spiritual ideal, flattering and encouraging those whose model he is meant to be. [Exactly, that is, as *Don Quixote* does.] . . . This shield and its device constitute an iconographical instance of extraordinary importance in the late Middle Ages, unique in its combination of rarity, elaboration, and focal position in the work as a whole. For the Middle Ages, the basic figurative meanings of armor, and especially helmet and shield, were found in Ephesians, chapter 6 . . ." (pp. 177, 181) But words have ceased to have real meanings, here. How can a critic write of a poem, in so shellshocked a state of scholarly dementia?

Then follows the Donald R. Howard essay, also re-

printed in the Fox collection, and after this comes
Charles Moorman's incredible "Myth and Medieval
Literature: *Sir Gawain and the Green Knight.*" It
would be hard for me to fairly characterize Mr. Moor-
man's weird analysis; the heart of it is the following,
which speaks, unfortunately, for itself:

> The *Gawain* poet, I maintain, is presenting us,
> within a deliberately limited form, a microcosm,
> or better said, a semi-allegorical presentation of
> the whole history and meaning of the Round
> Table. Morgan attempts reform; Gawain fails in
> keeping faith with Bercilak; treacherous Guine-
> vere remains alive. The form of the poem is thus
> quite consciously limited in time and in space in
> order to facilitate a unified and complete presen-
> tation of the progress of the Round Table; only
> in a single, complete adventure could the poet
> achieve any unified design which would reflect the
> whole of the tragedy. In this sense the poem is
> semi-allegorical in method . . .
>
>   *(p. 230—and not a word of it is invented)*

Mr. Burrow's *A Reading* . . . , referred to earlier, is
less harmful than the sort of thing just cited. It has a
dutiful, grade-school tone: "The most remarkable fea-
ture of this description, it seems to me, is its richness
and variety of suggestion. . . . The first view of any hero
helps to establish our sense of the relationship existing
between him and the society to which he belongs (*Ham-
let* provides an obvious example), and this relationship
is usually a matter of some importance. . . . It is as if
the Green Knight offers peace with one hand and war
with the other." (pp. 13, 8, 17) But he is also capable
of saying that Gawain's "proposal is *debated* by the
nobles before it is accepted by the king" (p. 11; my
italics), when as the poet indicates, the court, stunned
and incapacitated for decision-making of any kind,
merely buzzes a moment and then agrees, yes, yes, oh
quite right.

The knights whispered, buzzed,
Then all
In a voice said it was
For Gawain; the king should halt.

(Lines 362–365)

And Mr. Burrow listens to himself with so little atten-
tion that he can say, at one moment, "These elaborate
exchanges suggest that Gawain is entering into a sol-
emn quasi-legal agreement" (p. 23), and later on that
"Gawain's oath to the Green Knight is not entirely
solemn, and this casts a shadow of doubt across his
obligations" (p. 161). He can tell us, astonishingly, that
"When Gawain reaches the Green Chapel, for exam-
ple, he is decked out like a savage with talismans of
every description." (p. 178) It seems more usually dull,
only academically pompous, to observe that "The ge-
ography of Arthurian romance is, like its history and
its chronology, notoriously irresponsible" (p. 176), but
it seems to me that this is no less dangerous to the
student—who after all reads criticism in order to *learn,*
to be *informed,* to be *enlightened.* (I suspect, after sev-
eral decades of reading this sort of thing, that most of
these critics publish in order not to perish.) What true
learning is there in something like the following: "It
is not difficult, for example, to hear the voice of the
Preacher in the speech which he [the green knight]
makes after proposing his game and receiving no
reply . . . In these words one sees the court, for a
moment, exactly as one might see it in a Morality
Play, a Tragedy of Princes, or an 'ubi sunt' lyric . . ."
(p. 26)

Pedantry run mad can I hope be dismissed, with
simple replication of two notes from the Tolkien/Gor-
don/Davis text, those to line 879, *bleeaunt,* and to line
2316, *spenne-fote*:

> *bleeaunt.* Here a rich fabric, but in line 1928 ap-
> plied to a garment. The etymology and sense-
> development are uncertain. The form *bliaut* was

used in French as early as the twelfth century for a long over-tunic, worn by both sexes (see especially J. Evans, *Dress in Medieval France*, pp. 5 ff. and pls. 7, 10); it does not seem to have been used for a fabric as well. In Anglo-Norman the ending was replaced by *-ant*, *-aunt*, proper to the present participle (e.g., *bliaunt* in the Anglo-Norman *Bevis of Hampton* lines 738, 745), perhaps in part because *u* and *n* were indistinguishable in most manuscripts. The form with *n* appears also in Welsh and Middle Low German, but High German and Icelandic have that without *n*. Middle English usually has the *-n*-type, but the other also occurs, *e.g.*, *blyot* in *Parlement of Thre Ages* line 482.

We cannot tell how far the shape of the *bleaunt* in fourteenth-century England preserved that of the twelfth-century French *bliaut*. J. L. Nevinson, in *Medieval England* chapter IX, writes: "As might be expected, there are archaisms in *Sir Gawain and the Green Knight* such as the trailing *bliaut* worn indoors with a surcoat and a hood hanging on the shoulder" (p. 308). Yet from his attitude to armour and architecture the poet seems unlikely to have intended archaism in costume. It may be that the word had acquired a more general sense of "robe," which it might easily do from the use of the cloth for mantles, as here; cf. also *Sir Tristem* line 410: "In o robe . . . of a blihand broun."

spenne-fote. O.E.D. has "with feet close together," deriving *spenne* from Old Norse spenna, a verb, "clasp"; see *spenet* and *spenne* in glossary, and note on line 1074. J. H. Smith (*M.L.N.* xlix [1934], 462–463) shows that jumping with the feet together is standard practice in the broad jump, and cites French parallels with *ioint les piez* and the like. Yet similar words meaning "kick" exist in continental Germanic languages—Middle Dutch *spinnevoeten,* Low German *spinnefoten,* Modern Frisian *spinfoetsje*—which it would seem can hardly be unconnected, though no relation is apparent.

To turn back, briefly, from pedantry to poetry. No one can produce, in modern English, exact sound equivalents of the *Gawain*-poet's rugged Northern speech.

> Quat! hit clatered in þe clyff, as hit cleue schulde,
> As one vpon a gryndelston hade grounden a syþe.
> What! hit wharred and whette, as water at a mulne;
> What! hit rusched and ronge, rawþe to here.

> What! It clattered on the cliff, as if
> To split it, like a grindstone grinding a scythe.
> What! It whirred like water at a mill.
> What! It rushed and it rang, and it sang
> Miserably.

> *(Lines 2201–2205)*

The modern English is inevitably more effete: we have lost one kind of music, and learned another. One does what one can.

The bob-and-wheel has been, in about equal proportions, a delightful challenge and an affliction. My practice has been to come as close to the rhyming pattern of the original as I could, but never knowingly to sacrifice other qualities to the rhyme pattern. (I have been even freer with the meter.) I have rung a whole series of variations on the *Gawain*-poet's rather simple rhyming—everything from five (or even six) consecutive rhymes of the same sound, to the kind of part-rhyme, very much *rime faible,* of say lines 174–178, where *rider/decisive/bridle* form one rhyme, and *horse/caught up* another. I am proudest of such sequences as that in lines 55–59, where the *Gawain*-poet's pattern is quite closely followed, *castle/vassals/surpass him* rhyming in the odd-numbered lines, and *earth/worth* in the even-numbered ones; the metric, too, is the *Gawain*-poet's, or something close to it.

As always, I have tracked the original as closely as I could; my translation has the same number of lines as does the Middle English poem, the same strophic divisions, the bob-and-wheel at the same points, and it also follows the manuscript division into four parts (which I happen to think an integral and dramatic division of the poem). The metric used, except for the bob-and-wheel, is a four-stress line, with variable numbers of unstressed syllables—many more unstressed syllables, overall, than I have used in my Old English translations. This too follows the practice of the original, in which unstressed syllables are considerably more frequent than in Old English poetry. No one quite understands the Middle English alliterative line; I hope my echoing of it is—at least in this twentieth century—somewhat easier to follow.

I have occasionally, and always silently, woven footnotes into the text: I do not believe in footnoting poems, where it is humanly possible to avoid so doing. Nor do I think that the occurrence in the original manuscript of *Gawayn, Gawayne, Gawan, Gawen, Gauayn, Gauan, Wawan, Wawen, Wowen,* and *Wowayn* imposes on me any obligation whatever. Gawain is Gawain, here, throughout.

The easy availability of the paperback Tolkien/Gordon/Davis text, plus the penalty costs involved in setting Middle English in type, have made it impossible to set the original and my translation on facing pages. I wish it had not been impossible.

> —Burton Raffel
> March 1968–December 1969
> Natanya and Haifa, Israel
> Austin, Texas

INTRODUCTION

Tit for Tat:

A Fresh Look at *Sir Gawain and the Green Knight*

A huge green knight arrives at King Arthur's court and, swaggering arrogantly, challenges someone to behead him with the proviso that he can return the blow in a year and a day. Gawain accepts. The giant kneels and throws his green hair forward to bare a neck thick as a tree. A minute later his head is rolling across the ground. Laughing, the courtiers kick it like a ball, then watch, horrified, as the giant lurches to his feet and picks it up by the hair. His bloody lips tell Gawain to meet him at the Green Chapel in a year and a day. He promises the blow will be returned.

Almost a year later, on his way to the appointed meeting place, Gawain visits a castle and is persuaded by its lord, a seemingly friendly host, to stay for three nights. Unbeknownst to Gawain, the lord, Bercilak, is the Green Knight in another form. To entertain his guest, Bercilak suggests a game where they exchange winnings: whatever Bercilak kills in his day's hunting in exchange for what Gawain wins in the castle. Gawain, without realizing that it is a test of loyalty, agrees. While Bercilak hunts, his wife attempts to seduce Gawain. Gawain resists but finally allows her to give him her girdle, which she says will save his life. In the nightly exchange of winnings, he fails to turn it over to his host. Then, on the appointed day, Gawain meets the Green Knight and receives a light cut on his neck, which the Green Knight explains is for disloyalty. Realizing that the Green Knight and Bercilak are one and the same, Gawain is overcome by shame but blames his failure on women's perfidy. He returns to Arthur's court, wearing the girdle as a badge of his shame. The courtiers console him and swear that they too will wear girdles to keep their beloved knight company.

What is this all about? Scholars and critics have tended to hold violently opposed notions about the Green Knight, seeing him as either totally good or bad: as Christ or Devil, sadist or benevolent father. More recently, some critics like Benson have noted that he is both attractive and fearful without connecting this to the poem's larger psychological themes. If we look closely at the poem, we can see that the poet's ambivalence toward the Green Knight along with the unexplained challenge and equally illogical temptation and exchange are part of a single emotional field, which cries out for a psychological interpretation. The poem's enduring fascination lies in the way the poet holds powerful emotions of hate and love in balance and brings them into a psychologically deep and meaningful pattern specifically adapted to the feudal society in which the Gawain poet lived.

The opening of the poem is framed as a conflict between adolescent sons and a frightening father. When the Green Knight appears, he treats the court and king as children, taunting and shaming them. He swaggers up and down, looks insolently at the group on the high dais , and asks, "Where . . . / Is the lord of this company? I'd like to see him / In person and exchange some words" (ll. 224–26). When Arthur identifies himself as king, the Green Knight addresses him with the disrespectful "thou," and when Arthur offers to fight, the Green Knight humiliates him by remarking that he wouldn't think of fighting because "These benches are filled with beardless infants" (l. 280) The boyish king turns red with embarrassment.

The Green Knight's imposing physical appearance evokes in his audience both awe and fear, which enhance their feelings of childishness. The poet, however, leads the reader by stages from awe to sheer terror, from the merely exotic to the region of myth. He begins at the level of what is familiar by insisting that the Green Knight, though startlingly huge, is a perfect man, encouraging one's idealization of him as king, master or stern father. Once his superiority over the knights has been established, the poet moves on to his more primitive aspects—his grass green skin, bushlike beard, and long hair like a cape around his shoulders. His "tool," the powerful axe he carries, suggests vitality and phallic force.

The Green Knight's taunts and aggression both inhibit and stimulate the knights. A tension is built up between their wish to cut his head off and their fear of his power. The poet describes the beheading with almost voluptuous pleasure; the Green Knight throws back his lovely hair to bare his neck, and the blade enters his fair, bright flesh. Afterward the courtiers release their pent-up aggression by kicking the head around like a ball, laughing as blood spurts from the trunk. Unfortunately for them, the moment of triumph is short-lived. The spurned head becomes the agent of terror when the Green Knight, now hideously ugly, picks it up by the hair, and the mouth reminds Gawain that he must come for a return blow in a year and a day.

Though the poet nowhere identifies the Green Knight as Gawain's father—he is described as such in an earlier Medieval version—the Gawain poet has, with considerable richness and subtlety, evoked the same feelings as would a hostile confrontation between father and son leading up to the enactment of a parricidal fantasy. Precisely because the challenger is anonymous, and the challenge without reason, the reader can identify, without excessive guilt, with the aggression and humiliation that culminate in the beheading.

When a year has almost passed, Gawain sets out as he promised. After fighting off numerous monsters, enduring foul weather and praying to the Virgin Mary for help, he spots Bercilak's beautiful white castle. The host's remarkably kind and admiring treatment of Gawain offers a direct contrast to the scene of humiliation and shame at Arthur's court. Gawain's youthful beauty is praised: "And all at once it seemed to be Spring, / As his face shone, and that fair robe / Glistened with color" (ll. 865–67). Now he is even praised for his conversation and all present are eager to learn "the meaning / Of manners . . . the soothing of lovers' hurts" (ll. 924–25, 927). Bercilak is cordiality itself, sates Gawain's hunger, warms and feeds him, then proposes the friendly game of exchanging winnings.

It seems like a natural continuation of the fantasy of a loving castle-home when a beautiful woman appears. But the lady has a shadow; she is accompanied by a repulsive crone suggesting that seductive beauty has a reverse side—a point that foreshadows the misogyny at the poem's end. The verse builds up a counterpoint of desire and revulsion: "Rich red cheeks on the one, rough / and wrinkled jowls on the other" (ll. 952–53). The alluring brightness of the young one's breast "whiter than snow" (l. 956) is contrasted with the wrappings hiding the other's from sight. Her ugly guardian reminds the reader that the lady is at once the most desirable and the most forbidden, the wife of Gawain's host. In earlier Medieval romances and folktales the host was generally a cruel boor if not an actual ogre, and the knight either was chaste out of fear or felt justified about tricking the host out of his wife. But because here the temptation takes place within the context of Bercilak's fatherly concern for Gawain, the poet is able to add psychological depth, developing the conflict between Gawain's feelings of gratitude and loyalty and his sexual desire.

The temptation scenes that follow explore both his desire and his reluctance. Their artistry lies in the subtlety and variety of feelings they evoke. Gawain can't help desiring the beautiful creature but he admires his host and feels a sense of loyalty. The struggle between yearning and inhibition paralyzes him and makes him almost comically helpless before the lady's advances. In the first temptation scene, Gawain is reduced to pretending to sleep when he sees the lady sneak into his room. Later in the same scene, he lies motionless while she assures him that no one is around, the door is locked and he is welcome to her body. At this point, however, he thinks of his coming encounter with the Green Knight and desire vanishes. All he manages to do is give her a goodbye kiss, which he will dutifully return to his host at the night's exchange of winnings. If this is a fantasy of seduction by the mother, it also suggests the anxiety caused by a possible fulfillment of such a fantasy.

After the first temptation, we see Bercilak killing and cutting up a deer. He presents it to Gawain that night, reinforcing Gawain's constraining fear of dismemberment and death. We are made to sense a connection between Gawain's yielding to the lady and possible retaliation by her husband. But for now, Gawain only presents him with the kiss that the lady gave him in parting.

During a second day of temptation, the lady teases Gawain for forgetting her lesson in kissing and prods him to make love to her. He gallantly tells her his lips are hers to command but declines to go further. That night, after his hunt, the lord turns up with a boar's head, which Gawain receives with horror. The decapitated boar suggests, even more strongly than the deer, that it is a foreshadowing of the coming blow and the exchange of winnings, a warning.

In the third temptation scene, Gawain's fear isn't enough to restrain him in the face of the lady's increased seductiveness. She arrives dressed in furs, her breasts bare, and starts kissing him. Now he is saved only by thinking of another woman—the Virgin Mary—whose knight he is. Mary is the most exalted and loving mother who can be imagined. Her image provides better protection than any worldly sweetheart. While she doesn't offer sexual gratification, her care satisfies other needs, especially that of a child for the safety of a mother's embrace. She also helps Gawain overcome thoughts of rivalry with a superior

male. She is a virgin. No man has sexual priority with
her, and she is totally devoted to worshipping her son.
In addition, there is no guilt connected with loving
her. It is no accident that Gawain has her device on
his shield.

In parting from Bercilak's wife, Gawain accepts her
girdle as a token because she insists it will save his
life. Though it serves as a reminder of his desire, he
can accept it because for the moment his inhibitions
have quieted. The gift itself will protect him.

The Gawain poet doesn't satisfy the incestuous wish
in the structure of the poem. Instead he humiliates
the hero for forgetting himself enough to take the gir-
dle and for keeping it secret from his host instead of
turning it over in the exchange. The girdle episode
should be taken as an allusion to a solution to emo-
tional conflict common to folk- or fairy tales in which
a young hero receives a protective gift from a giant's
wife or daughter. As an episode in a familial drama,
it suggests the wish to be protected by the mother
from the father's anger while yet deceiving him.

The Gawain poet's joining of the beheading game
and the temptation—separate in all but one early
version—enables the poet to present with great econ-
omy a whole range of feelings both positive and nega-
tive toward paternal authority. These feelings come to
a head when Gawain and the Green Knight meet at
the Green Chapel.

Fear is uppermost as Gawain approaches their
meeting place. He asks directions and is warned to
avoid the ferocious giant, who kills all who pass.
Though his guide's assertion that the giant has been
around since ancient times doesn't fit logically with
the plot, the allusion to myth and folktale reminds us
that the emotions he arouses are ancient and known
to all.

Arriving at the appointed place, Gawain wonders if
it is the site of devilish rites. This is partially a projec-
tion of his guilty conscience. He doesn't want to admit
to himself that he has been disloyal, has held back the

girdle and told an untruth. It's much easier to see the Devil in the landscape. The Green Knight confronts Gawain and taunts him, feinting with his axe and finally dealing the long expected return blow. To Gawain's and our surprise, it merely breaks the skin. Gawain then learns that his opponent and his host are one and the same. His humiliation continues as the Green Knight explains that the wound he received is for disloyalty in taking the girdle. Though at this point the more benign persona of Bercilak takes over and praises Gawain as a perfect paladin, Gawain is overcome with shame and denounces himself as sinful.

But the bulk of his anger is directed outward in a misogynistic tirade to the effect that men have been deceived by women since Adam, and since women are not to be trusted, Gawain should be excused. This rant has mystified critics. But it is quite easily understood in the context of his struggle with his own desire and his failure to be the Virgin Mary's perfect Christian Knight. His shame at his weakness is projected onto what tempted him—woman.

Gawain's disgust at the woman who tempted him is mirrored symbolically in his reaction to the Green Chapel. When he first arrives, he sees a swelling mound with a hole at one end and a stream bubbling by, and observes that the Devil might well recite his prayers there. He's struck by the age and ugliness of the place, an old cave, "a crevice in crag," overgrown with grass (l. 2183). His strong reaction suggests a missing association. Within the poem the closest parallel is his sexual disgust at the sight of the old crone.

The association of mound hole and woman is certainly not unique to the Gawain poet. The earth's mysterious holes and caves are analogous to the woman's genitals and hidden inner organs. Their association with the Devil is a logical result of Medieval Christian attitudes toward sex where "putting the Devil in hell" could be a jocular reference to intercourse.

Gawain's negative associations to the mound/hole anticipate his misogynistic outburst. But his dread is more elemental and immediate than that rationalization. The author finally reveals that Morgan le Fay, a powerful sorceress hostile to Arthur's court, was behind the beheading game. This takes the process a step further: woman is responsible not just for men's sinful thoughts but for their aggression toward one another. Gawain's dread, his misogyny and Morgan's responsibility are all part of a pattern in which the anger generated among rivalrous men is displaced onto women in a way that reinforces the filial and societal bonds among men. Gawain returns to court to found a masculine order of shame with his brother knights; the surreptitiously obtained girdle is its badge.

Sir Gawain and the Green Knight reaffirms the power of the father. It dramatizes the way allegiance to the father and his values is set up in the child's mind through a mixture of intimidation and caring. It is part of the Gawain poet's mature artistry that he insists on unity of personality: the caring Bercilak and the fearsome Green Knight are aspects of the same man. Gawain's conflict over his adulterous longings invokes the incest taboo on which patriarchal society rests. The triangle of Bercilak, wife and Gawain repeats on a social level the earlier family triangle of father, mother and son. Unlike Sophocles, the Gawain poet isn't writing about the dream of incest fulfilled and tragically punished. He is writing about wishes that are coaxed out by temptation and then rejected and consciously suppressed.

Though the Gawain poet fully explores the impulses of humiliated rage and rivalry that lead men to violence (in the beheading) or disloyalty (in the seduction), conflict within the poem is resolved in favor of authority—whether the fixed structure of feudal loyalty or the hierarchical frame of religion. The poet underscores his stance by his use of Christian symbols. The beheading and the return blow are fitted into the Christian calendar: they fall on New Year's Day, the Christian Feast of the Circumcision when Christ, God's Son, entered the covenant, ensuring God of his absolute submission by enduring the mutilation of his genitals.

But the poem does more than dramatize the formation of an individual conscience through identification with the father and a chauvinistic contempt for women. It shows us how this particular type of conscience and set of attitudes meshed with the feudal Christian society in which the Gawain poet lived. French feudal society was built on assemblies of noble houses in which often only the eldest son was allowed to marry. Wandering in turbulent bands, the younger sons presented a constant danger to their married brothers. In this context the temptation—in which temptation is controlled by the lord—suggests an imaginative effort to domesticate a social threat. It is a poem of maturation through temptation and fear—a paradigm of the socialization of youth into family, morality and feudal society.

The story of Sir Gawain fascinated me as a graduate student and for years afterward. Every time I returned to it, I would be deeply impressed and absorbed by the beauty of the poet's images, and the verses that sent shivers down my back when the Green Knight came galloping into the castle hall. I responded to the human conflicts. But there were things that bothered me too, particularly the need to blame women for men's troubles. It seemed to set the direction for centuries of patriarchal oppression. I felt inspired to try a modern version of the tale.

In my novel *The Beheading Game*, I imagine a gay playwright, Ren, who loves the excitement and drama of the poem but wants to shake up the patriarchal model that he feels excludes him. He creates a cross-gendered version with Gawain played by a feisty woman who takes Bercilak's lady to task for her willingness to be used as a temptress of young men. At the same time the familial triangle plays out in Ren's everyday life as he confronts a modern version of the Green Knight, his lover Jack's father, who tries to deny Ren access to his severely ill son. Jack cannot bring himself to be disloyal to the older man, but Ren finds an ingenious way to thwart the father and care for his lover. Ren may not be able to solve all his problems in life, but his play is a rousing success. Its comic finale results in a more equal sharing of power between the sexes and between young and old and a new model of heroism in which bedpans are more important than battles and loyalty must be deserved.

A masterpiece like *Sir Gawain* is so rich and operates on so many levels that it continues to be relevant long after its creation and stimulates us not only to enjoy and interpret it but to use it as jumping off place for our own tales.

HONY SOYT QUI MAL PENCE

—Brenda Webster

SIR GAWAIN
AND THE
GREEN KNIGHT

PART ONE

Once the siege and assault had done for Troy,
And the city was smashed, burned to ashes,
The traitor whose tricks had taken Troy
For the Greeks, Aeneas the noble, was exiled
For Achilles' death, for concealing his killer,   *5*
And he and his tribe made themselves lords
Of the western islands, rulers of provinces,
And rich: high-handed Romulus made Rome
Out of nothing, built it high and blessed it
With his name, the name we know; and Tirrus   *10*
Father of Tuscan founded towns;
And the Lombards planted a land; and Brutus
Split the sea, sailed from France
To England and opened cities on slopes
                               And hills,   *15*
           Where war and marvels
           Take turns with peace,
           Where sometimes lightning trouble
           Has struck, and sometimes soft ease.

And noble Brutus' Britain grew rich   *20*
In battle-bold knights, who loved to fight
And fought, and often brought pain to their people.
Far more than in any land in the world
Wonderful things have been worked in England.

25 But of all her kings Arthur was always
    Most glorious, as the tales tell—and knowing
    A strange adventure, told of Arthur
    And his knights, as surpassingly strange a tale
    As even Britain has spawned, I'll tell it
30 Here and now, as I've heard it told,
    If you'd like to listen to the poem I'll read,
                              Spun
                Out of ancient stories
                Set down by honest men
35   With bold words
                And faithful pens.

    At Christmas the king held court at Camelot,
    Surrounded by gracious lords, worthy
    Knights of the Round Table, brothers in arms,
40 Reveling in that rich pleasure. Noble
    Knights day after day rode
    In tourneys, jousted gallant and well,
    Then galloped to court, and sang, and danced—
    For Camelot's Christmas feast was fifteen
45 Days, as full of food and laughter
    As feasting could be made, loud and happy
    And glorious to listen to, noisy days,
    Dancing nights, lords and ladies
    Rejoicing in their rooms, and in Arthur's castle,
50 Coming together in the height of delight,
    The most famous warriors of Christ our King,
    And the loveliest ladies in the world, and Arthur
    The noblest of rulers, reigning in his court.
    It was springtime in Camelot, in the Christmas snow,
55   In that castle
                Most blessed on earth,
                With the best of vassals
                And a king of such worth
                That no time will surpass him.

60 With the New Year drawing close, courtiers
    And ladies sat to a double feast;
    Mass had been sung in the chapel, the king
    And his knights came to the hall, and priests

And laymen called "Noël! Noël!"
And shouted and sang, and nobles ran   65
With New Year's presents in their hands, noisily
Passing in a crowd, calling "Presents!
Presents!" and loudly disputing gifts,
While ladies laughed when kisses were lost
(And whoever won them found it hard to weep),   70
And till dinnertime came they ran and laughed;
Then they washed and sat at that stately table,
The noblest nearest their lord, and his queen,
Guenevere the gay, seated in their midst:
Arranged around that priceless table   75
Fringed with silk, with silk hung
Over their heads, and behind them velvet
Carpets, embroidered rugs, studded
With jewels as rich as an emperor's ransom—
                                   And the queen   80
                    Watching with shining
                    Gray eyes, seemed
                    As beautiful a lady
                    As a man could have seen.

Yet Arthur, boisterous and merry as a boy,   85
Refused to eat till the others were served:
His blood ran young, and his brain was restless,
And he liked to be gay, he hated lying
About or sitting long at a time.
And a point of honor held him back,   90
A vow he had taken and meant to keep,
Not to be seated at a festive table
Until he'd been told a tale of adventures
Or marvels, some mighty story to remember
Of princes, of battles, of perils or wonders,   95
Or a courtly visitor had begged some knight
Of the Round Table to rise and ride in combat,
Fight for his life, man against man,
As fate determined. Wherever he held
His court the king was ruled by this custom,   100
Whenever he sat with his knights around him
                                   And feasted.

His face proud
He remained on his feet,
105 And his laughter was loud
As he waited his New Year's treat.

So the fearless king stood in front of his table,
Talking of elegant trifles. And Gawain
The good sat beside Guenevere, and Agravaine
110 Of the hard hands on her other side,
Both Arthur's nephews, faithful knights,
And Bishop Bawdune at the king's right
And Urian's son Ywain with him.
This central table sat high in luxury
115 And around them lesser knights in rows.
With a flaring crack of trumpets the feast
Began, trumpets all hung with bright banners,
And drums beat, and glorious bagpipes
Rumbled and shrilled their quick-step tunes,
120 And hearts beat quick with the music. At the signal
Rare and delicate dishes were served,
And venison in great slabs, and so many platters
That there was almost no place to set them in front of
The guests, broths and stews in overflowing
125   Abundance.
All ate as they pleased
And as much as they wanted,
A dozen dishes apiece,
And beer and wine flowed free.

130 I've nothing more to tell of their feasting:
Any fool knows with what splendor they were fed.
And to send the prince to his dinner, a different
Sound approached—the trumpets and pipes
Were barely still, the drums silent,
135 The first dishes set in place,
When a ghastly knight sprang through the door,
Huge, taller than men stand, so square
And thick from neck to knee, thighs
So broad around, legs so long,
140 He seemed half an ogre, a giant,
But clearly the biggest creature in the world

And the fairest, the gayest for his size, as thin
In the waist, as flat in the belly, as his back
And chest were grim and immense, from cheek
To chin fine and elegant, with an easy   *145*
                         Grace
                    And stunning the court
                    With the color of his race:
                    A fiery, snorting
                    Fellow, and his hands were green, and   *150*
                      his face.

And his armor, and his shirt, were green, all green:
A short tight tunic, worn close, and a merry
Mantle, sewn-in with fur that rippled
As he rode, trimmed rich at the edges with bright
White ermine, both his mantle and the hood thrown *155*
  low
On his back, below his flowing hair;
And his smooth-webbed stockings, stretched taut
  on his legs,
Were green, all striped with embroidered silk,
And his shining spurs were gold, and he wore
No shoes, rode peacefully to that prince's court. *160*
Everything about him was an elegant green,
From the colored bands on his belt to the jewels
Set in his clothes and his saddle, woven
Around with silk designs: birds
And butterflies flew in that embroidery, beautifully *165*
Worked and fine, decorated in green
And with gold scattered across them. His horse's
Armor was enameled, and the saddle and its straps
And the bit in its teeth were green, and the stirrups
For that knight's feet were green, and his saddle *170*
Horn, and the shining leather hung
From the saddle, glittering and gleaming with green
Stones, and his stallion too, as green
                         As its rider,
                    A huge horse,   *175*
                    Headstrong, decisive

And quick, but caught up
By his hand's touch on the bridle.

His clothes and his armor were glorious, this green
180 Knight, his hair the color of his horse
And waving down his shoulders. A beard
As thick as a bramble-bush grew from his chin
And fell in front as far as the hair
In back, hair and beard cut
185 At the elbow, like a king's hooded cape
Enclosing his neck and half his arms;
And his horse's mane hung long, combed
And curled, braided strand for strand
With gold thread, a strand of green hair,
190 Another of gold; and his forelock, and his tail
Were braided to match, bound in place
With a green band, dotted with precious
Stones the length of that flowing tail,
Then laced with an elaborate knot, and strung
195 With dozens of bright gold bells that rang
As he rode—and rider, and horse, stranger
Than anything seen on earth, before
                         That day.
           He seemed to glow
200   Like lightning, they say
           Who were there: who could know
           The force of his blows?

And yet he wore no helmet, no mail-shirt,
No neck-armor, nothing against steel or arrow,
205 Nor carried a shield nor swung a spear,
Had only a branch of holly in one hand
(Holly that grows greenest when the woods are
    bare)
And an axe in the other, monstrous, huge,
A vicious weapon four feet wide,
210 Hammered of green steel, and of gold,
With a polished blade, a bright cutting
Edge, and long, and stropped like a razor
Ready to shear, and his hand held it
By a thick staff, strong and straight

And wound round with iron at the end;   215
It was carved with lovely green symbols and designs
And hung by a strap run through the head
And down the handle, looped around
And tied with delicate tassels and embroidered
Buttons, green and rich. This knight   220
Stalked in the door and through the hall
To Arthur's high table, afraid of no one,
Greeting no one, ignoring them all.
And when he spoke: "Where," he said,
"Is the lord of this company? I'd like to see him   225
In person and exchange some words." He stared
                              At the knights,
          Rolling his eyes up
          And down, then stopped
          And squinted, hunting the knight   230
          Of noblest renown.

And they themselves sat and stared,
Wondering, bewildered, what it meant that a knight
And his horse could have such a color, could grow
As green as grass, or greener! and glow   235
Brighter than emerald enamel and gold.
And those who were standing watched, and walked
Carefully near him, not knowing what he'd do—
They'd all seen wonders, but nothing like this.
And some said he was witchcraft, a phantom,   240
And were afraid to answer him, then gasped at his
     voice
And trembled, sitting motionless in that noble
Hall, silent as stones, as corpses;
All speech was swept away as if sleep
                              Had dropped   245
          From the sky—but some
          Surely stopped
          Their tongues in courtesy, to do honor
          To Arthur, whose words should come
             first.

And Arthur stood watching the strange arrival   250

And greeted him gravely (for he knew nothing of
      fear)
And said, "Sir, you are welcome in my house,
For I am Arthur and I rule this court.
Step down from your horse and stay, let me pray
      you,
255 And whatever you've come for can be talked of
      afterward."
"No, God help me," said the green man, "I have
No interest in lingering here! Yet you
And your court are so famous, prince, and your
      castle
And your knights are praised so widely—the proud-
      est,
260 The boldest soldiers to sit on a horse,
The bravest and best of men, eager
To compete in noble games—and your courtesy
Is told in such terms, that I came to see
If these tales were true. You can surely tell
265 By this branch here in my hand that I've come
In peace, not seeking, not giving offense:
Had I ridden with my men, intending to fight,
I've a helmet and mail-shirt at home, and a shield,
And a sharp spear, shining bright,
270 And other weapons meant for war.
I intend no war, what I wear is in peace.
And if Arthur is as brave as his fame, in the name
Of this Christmas season you'll grant me the sport
                                    I've come for."

275   And Arthur replied,
             "Your wish is done, sir.
             If you've come to fight
             We'll fight and not run, sir."

"No, not fighting: believe me, prince.
280 These benches are filled with beardless infants.
Wearing my armor, riding to war,
There's no muscle in this hall to match me. It's a
      game
I want to play, a Christmas sport

For the season. Your court sings of its daring:
If they'll dare it, any of these eager knights,   285
Rise so boldly, so fierce, so wild,
And give a blow and take a blow,
I'll offer this noble axe and let them
Swing its weight as they like, and I'll sit
Without armor and invite them to strike as they   290
    please.
Anyone with the nerve to try it, take
This axe, here. Hurry, I'm waiting!
Take it and keep it, my gift forever,
And give me a well-aimed stroke, and agree
To accept another in payment, when my turn   295
                    Arrives,
            But not now: a year
            And a day will be time
            Enough. So: is anyone here
            Able to rise?"   300

If he'd stunned them at first, they sat stiller, now,
All who followed Arthur, noble
And knave. That knight swiveled in his saddle,
His eyes rolling fierce and red,
And he wrinkled his bristling brows, gleaming   305
Green, and switched his beard from side
To side— And no one rose— And he reared
Like a lord, and yelped, and laughed, and said:
"Hah! Is this Arthur's house, hailed
Across the world, that fabled court?   310
Where have your conquests gone to, and your pride,
Where is your anger, and those awesome boasts?
And now the Round Table's fame and its feasting
Are done, thrown down at the sound of one man's
Words—and you sit there shaking—at words!"   315
And he laughed so loud that Arthur winced,
His fair face flooded hot with shame,
                                And his cheeks;
            He flared as angry as wind,
            And all his people   320

Burned. And the bold king
Strode toward the green

Knight: "By God, fellow, this is foolish
Stuff—but you've asked for folly, and folly
325 You'll get! No one's afraid of your nonsense:
For God's sake, give me your axe, I'll grant
Your request!" Light and fast, he ran
And clasped the green knight's hand. And proudly
The green man dismounts. And Arthur lifts
330 The axe, and whips it about, gripping it
Firm in his fists, grim, determined.
That haughty knight stood huge at his side,
A head and more the tallest in the hall;
Stroking his beard, his face set
335 And still, he quietly pulled down his coat,
As indifferent to Arthur swishing his axe
As if the king were a waiter carrying
                                    Wine.

Gawain was seated near
340   The queen; he leaned
Forward: "Hear me,
My lord. Let this challenge be mine."

Then Gawain bowed to the king. "Release me,
My liege, from this bench, and let me come to you,
345 Permit me to rise without discourtesy,
And without displeasing your queen. Let me come
To counsel you, here in your noble court.
It seems wrong—everyone knows how wrong—
When a challenge like this rings through your hall
350 To take it yourself, though your spirit longs
For battle. Think of your bold knights,
Bursting to fight, as ready and willing
As men can be: defer to their needs.
And I am the slightest, the dullest of them all;
355 My life the least, my death no loss—
My only worth is you, my royal
Uncle, all my virtue is through you.
And this foolish business fits my station,
Not yours: let me play this green man's game.

If I ask too boldly, may this court declare me   360
               At fault."
        The knights whispered, buzzed,
        Then all
        In a voice said it was
        For Gawain; the king should halt.   365

Then Arthur ordered his knight to rise,
And Gawain rose and came quickly
To the king, and kneeled, and accepted the green
   man's
Axe as Arthur yielded it, lifting
His hands to bring God to Gawain, commanding   370
That heart and hand must be steady and strong.
"Be careful, cousin," said the king, "to strike
But once; offer exactly what he asks
And his stroke will be easier to stand." Axe
In hand Gawain approached the green man,   375
Who waited patient, calm, unmoving.
Then he spoke to the knight: "Before we proceed,
Friend, we ought to make everything clear.
And I ask you, first, your name: speak it
Openly, and speak the truth." "In truth   380
It is Gawain who offers this stroke, and agrees,
No matter what happens, to accept a stroke
From you, in exactly a year, with whatever
Weapon you choose—from you, and only
               From you!"   385
        The green man smiled:
        "Sir Gawain, no one could do
        What you'll do, and delight me
        More—no man alive.

"By God," he swore, "Sir Gawain, I'm glad   390
To have what I wanted at your hands. You've spoken
Our bargain beautifully, and spoken it fair,
And omitted nothing I asked the king
Except, knight, your word to seek me
Yourself, to come to me there where I am,   395
At home on this earth, and to take the same
Reward you'll give me today in this court."

"And where will you be?" asked Gawain. "Where
Is your home? By God, I've never heard
400 Of your castle, or you, or your court, or your name.
Tell me, teach me, give me your name,
And I'll come to you, however hard the road,
Wherever you are: I swear on my word."
"That's oath enough, at Christmas," said the green
 man,
405 "I need no more. Once you've swung my axe
Neatly and well, there'll be time to tell you
Where my home is and my house, and to tell you
 my name,
And you'll test my castle, and me, and keep
Your word. And perhaps I'll say nothing, once
410 You've struck, which is better for you, you could
 stay
Here with your king and not hunt my door—
                              But stop!
            Take my good axe
            And show me a chop."
415   "Exactly as you ask,"
            Said Gawain, ready to strop.

Still smiling, the green man bowed, and bent
His head a bit, baring his neck,
His lovely long hair tossed back, leaving
420 The naked flesh open, exposed.
Gawain hefted the axe, swung it high
In both hands, balancing his left foot in front of him,
Then quickly brought it down. The blade
Cut through bones and skin and fair
425 White flesh, split the green man's neck
So swiftly that its edge slashed the ground.
And the head fell to the earth, rolled
On the floor, and the knights kicked it with their
 feet:
The body spurted blood, gleaming
430 Red on green skin—but the green man stood
A moment, not staggering, not falling, then sprang

On strong legs and roughly reached through thrash-
   ing
Feet, claimed his lovely head,
And carrying it to his horse caught the bridle,
Stepped in the stirrups and mounted, holding   435
His head by its long green hair, sitting
High and steady in the saddle as though nothing
Had happened. But he sat there headless, for every-
   one
                      To see,
      Twisting his bloody, severed   440
      Stump. And the knights were wary,
      Afraid before he ever
      Opened that mouth to speak.

And he held that head high, slowly turning
Its face toward Arthur and the noblest of his   445
   knights,
And it lifted its lids and stared with wide eyes
And moved its lips and spoke, saying:
"Gawain, be ready to ride as you promised;
Hunt me well until you find me—
As you swore to, here in this hall, heard   450
By these knights. Find the green chapel, come
To take what you've given, a quick and proper
Greeting for a New Year's Day. Many men
Know the knight of the green chapel:
Seek me, and nothing can keep you from me.   455
Then come! or be called a coward forever."
With a violent rush he turned the reins
And galloped from the hall, his head in his hands;
His horse's hooves struck fire on the stone.
And where he rode to no one knew,   460
No more than they'd known from where he came.
                    And then?
      Arthur and Gawain grinned
      At the joke, and laughed at the green
      man,
      Though those who had seen him   465
      Knew miracles had been sent.

Arthur's heart whirled in wonder,
Yet he showed nothing, turned to his beautiful
Queen and spoke courteously, but loud:
470 "My love, let nothing of this disturb you.
These are things right and proper
For Christmas, and for courtly ladies and their
      knights,
Miming and plays, carols and laughter.
But now I can dine, I admit it; the marvel
475 I awaited has come." Then he glanced toward
      Gawain:
"Sir," he said slowly, "hang up
Your axe: it has cut enough for one night."
And servants hung it high against
A tapestry, a trophy for everyone to stare at,
480 True evidence of marvelous things.
Then knights and ladies returned to table,
And Arthur and Gawain, and good men served
      them
Double portions, as rank demanded.
They ate and drank and listened and watched
485 And the day was delight, and was long, and was
      finally

                              Done.
               And now, Gawain: think.
               Danger is yours to overcome
               And this game brings you
490   Danger. Can the game be won?

PART TWO

The green man began Arthur's New Year
With the marvels he loved to hear of. But the men
Of the Round Table sat silent at their meat, stuffed,
Now, with grim business. Gawain
Enjoyed the beginning of that game, in his king's   *495*
Court, but no one would laugh at the end—
For men may be cheerful, mulling their wine,
But a year runs fast, and always runs different;
Start and finish are never the same.
So Christmas goes by, and all the swift year,   *500*
Each season racing after the other:
Christmas pursued by uncomfortable Lent,
Trying men's flesh with simple food
And with fish; then fair weather fights with foul,
Clouds fill the sky, the cold shrinks away,   *505*
Rain falls clear in warm showers,
And the flat earth opens into flowers
And fields and plains grow thick and green,
Birds start their nests and sing like angels
For love of soft summer, creeping across   *510*
                      The slopes;
        And hedgerows swell tall,
        And blossoms blow open,
        And glorious woods are all
        Echoing joy and hope.   *515*

And after summer's soft winds, Zephyrus
Whistles quietly with seeds and herbs,
Sprouting delightful plants, painted
Wet with dew falling from leaves,
520 Waiting to be warm in the bright sun.
Then autumn comes rushing, calling the plants
To watch for winter, to grow while they can;
And he dries the earth and drives dust
Swirling to the sky, and wild winds
525 Run to wrestle with the sun; leaves
Are thrown from trees and lie dead on the ground,
And green grass withers. And everything
Slender and new ripens and rots,
And a year runs away in passing days,
530 And winter winds back, as winter must,
                              Just so.
              Till the Michaelmas moon
              Promises snow—
              And Gawain soon
535   Recalls what he has to do.

But he stays with Arthur till All-Saints Day.
And the king makes a feast in his honor, the court
And their ladies merry around the Round Table,
Gracious knights and lovely women
540 Grieving for love of Gawain, but laughing
And drinking his name, smiling and joking
While their hearts sank gray and cold. And Gawain
Feasts, then sadly approaches his uncle
And speaks of his journey, and bluntly says:
545 "Lord of my life, I ask your leave.
You know my promise: I've no pleasure in retelling
    it,
Spelling my troubles, except just this:
Tomorrow I go to the green man and his axe,
Tomorrow without fail, as God guides me."
550 And the best of Arthur's knights came to him,
Iwain, and Eric, and many more,
Sir Dodinel de Sauvage, the Duke of Clarence,
Lancelot, and Lionel, and Lucan the Good,

Sir Bors, and Sir Bedivere—strong men, both—
And other proud knights, with Mador de la Port.   555
They came to the king, all of them, to counsel
Gawain, but their hearts were heavy. In secret
Thoughts, that day, Arthur's hall
Rang with silent lament, sorrow
For so good a man as Gawain, on so hard   560
                A quest.
         But Gawain only smiled:
         "Should I waste my time
         With fear? Whether pleasant or wild,
         Fate must be put to the test."   565

So he rested that day, then rose the next morning
And at dawn called for his armor. It was brought,
But first a rich red rug was spread
On the floor: gold armor gleamed where it lay.
Then Gawain stepped forward, took steel in his   570
   hands,
And over a doublet of Tharsia silk
Fastened a hood, tied at the neck
And lined inside with thick fur. Then hammered
Steel shoes were set on his feet, and his legs
Wrapped all around with well-hinged metal,   575
With armored knee-plates, polished bright
And fastened tight by golden cords;
Thigh-plates, elegant and thick, closed
Around his strong muscles, and were laced
In place. And then his mail-shirt, metal   580
Woven like silk, hung shimmering on his chest,
And polished arm-pieces, and beautifully bent
Elbow joints, and steel gloves,
And all the equipment he needed, and owned,
               For that ride,   585
         Draped with heraldic designs—
         And gold spurs on his feet,
         And his good sword at his side,
         And a sash belted neat.

And Gawain's gear shone rich, the smallest   590
Laces and loops glowing with gold.

Ready in armor, he stood at the altar
For mass to be chanted, then came to the king
And the assembled knights of Arthur's court,
595 And took courteous leave of lords and ladies,
Who kissed him, commended him to Christ, then
    walked him
There where Gringolet stood ready, his saddle
Of gleaming leather, hung with gold,
Studded with new nails, and a striped bridle,
600 Trimmed and tied with gold. And Gringolet's
Breast-plates, and shining saddle-skirts,
And tail-armor, and the cloth on his back, matched
His saddle-bows, all set on a background
Of rich gold nails that glittered like the sun.
605 Then Gawain lifted his lined helmet,
Sewn like steel, and quickly kissed it;
It sat high on his head, clasped behind,
With delicate embroidered silk on the neckband,
Decorated with jewels along its length
610 And with birds stitched on the seams, parrots
Perched among painted purple flowers,
And turtle doves, and lovers' knots
So thick that ladies could have sewn them for seven
                      Winters.
615   And around the top
            Of his helmet were a crop
            Of diamonds, brown and white, sprinkled
            In a magic knot.

Then they carried in his shield, striped with bright
    red;
620 A pentangle star, painted pure gold,
Shone at its center. He swings it by the belt,
Then tosses it across his neck. And the sign
Of that star, its perfect points, fitted
That prince, and I'll tell you how, though it hold up
625 This tale. Solomon shaped that star—
Triangles blended in triangles—as a symbol
Of truth, for each of its angles enfolds
The other, and fastens the other, five

In all and everywhere endless (and everywhere
In England called the infinite knot).   *630*
And Gawain wears it by right, on his bright
Armor, faithful five ways and each way
Five times, a noble knight, as pure
As gold, as good as any knight in any gleaming
                                          Castle   *635*
            And worthy of that star,
            The noblest of men in asking
            And telling, the hardest
            For words to baffle.

His five senses were free of sin;   *640*
His five fingers never failed him;
And all his earthly hope was in Christ's
Five wounds on the cross, as our creed tells us;
And whenever he stood in battle his mind
Was fixed, above all things, on the five   *645*
Joys which Mary had of Jesus,
From which all his courage came—and was why
This fair knight had her face painted
Inside his shield, to stare at Heaven's
Queen and keep his courage high.   *650*
And the fifth of his fives was love and friendship
For other men, and freedom from sin,
And courtesy that never failed, and pity,
Greatest of knightly virtues—and these noble
Five were the firmest of all in his soul.   *655*
And all these fives met in one man,
Joined to each other, each without end,
Set in five perfect points
Wholly distinct, yet part of one whole
And that whole seamless, each angle open   *660*
And closed, wherever it end or begin.
And so the pentangle glowed on his shield,
Bright red gold across bright red stripes,
The holy pentangle, as careful scholars
                                          Call it.   *665*
            And Gawain was ready,
            And his lance steady

In front of him, wished them all
Farewell, and then rode from that hall.

670 He spurred his horse and rode strongly away;
Sparks flew from the stones. And Arthur's
Court watched him, and sighed, all Camelot
Sad at his fate, men saying
One to the other: "By Christ, what a crime
675 To lose Gawain, whose life was so noble!
How many men on this earth can match him?
Better to have been more prudent, to have made him
A duke before this could happen. He seemed
A brilliant leader, and could have been,
680 And had better been than this—his head
Lopped off by an elf, and only for pride.
What king has ever allowed such games,
Playing such stupid sport at Christmas!"
Warm tears rolled in their eyes
685 As they watched that lovely knight riding
                              Away.
              And he never delayed,
              Rode on his way;
              And books say
690   That he rode where men go astray.

And he rode through England, Sir Gawain, on God's
Behalf, though the ride was hardly a happy one.
He was often alone, at night, in places
Where the path ahead of him could please no one.
695 Only his horse rode with him, through woods
And hills, and the only voice he heard
Was God's, until he reached the north
Of Wales. The Anglesey Islands were always
To his left; he forded rivers near the highlands,
700 Crossing at Holy Head and landing
In the wilderness of Wirral Forest, where few men
Lived whom God or a good man could love.
And Gawain asked, as he rode, if anyone
He met had heard of a green man, or a green
705 Chapel, anywhere nearby, and everyone
Said no, never in their lives, neither seen

Nor heard of a man whom heaven had colored
                              Green.
                    Gawain's path
                    Wound through dreary scenes,   710
                    And his head leaned
                    First this way, then that, as he hunted
                         that chapel.

He climbed over cliffs in many strange lands,
Nowhere near home, friendless now.
And at every ford over every stream   715
He found himself facing enemies so foul
And wild that they forced him to fight for his life.
He met so many marvels in those hills
It is difficult to tell a tenth of it—dragons
Attacked him, and sometimes wolves, and satyrs,   720
And forest trolls, running out of rocks,
And bulls, and bears, and ivory-tusked boars,
And giant ogres leaping from crags.
His strength saved him, and his courage, and his
     faith
In God: he could have died a dozen times   725
Over. And the fighting was hard, but the foul
Winter was worse, so cold that rain
Froze before it could fall to earth;
Sleeping in his armor, sleet came close
To killing him, lying on open rock   730
Where icy rivers charged from mountains
And over his head icicles hung,
Sharp and hard. In danger and hardship
Gawain stayed alone, riding until Christmas
                              Eve,   735
                    When he prayed to Mary
                    To end his grief,
                    To guide his weary
                    Steps to relief.

Next morning, more cheerful, he rode down a hill   740
To a deep forest, incredibly wild,
Set into mountains and surrounded by hundreds
Of huge gray oaks. Hazel and hawthorn

Were snarled and tangled together, and shaggy
745 Moss hung everywhere in ragged clumps;
And sad birds sat on the bare
Branches, piping pitifully in the cold.
Gawain hurried his horse, crossed swamps
And mires and bogs, acres of mud,
750 Afraid, now, that he'd lost all chance
Of hearing Christmas mass and honoring
Mary's son, born to end
Our sorrow; and sighing, he said: "Oh Lord,
Oh Mary, gentlest Mother and dear,
755 I beg you to send me some lodging, to let me
Hear mass before morning; I ask meekly,
And in proof pray swiftly my pater, my ave,
                               My creed."
              He prayed as he rode,
760   And wept for misdeeds,
              And shaped the sign of the cross
              And called Christ in his need.

Three times he shaped that sign, and suddenly,
On a hill above a field, set deep
765 Among massive trees, he saw a moat
And a castle—the loveliest ever owned,
In the middle of a meadow, with woods and lawns
And a thick palisade fence, and grass
And grounds running more than two miles. And
    Gawain
770 Stared at those stone walls glittering
Through tall white oaks, towering around
A steep moat, and removing his helmet
Gave courteous thanks to Jesus and Julian,
Patron of travelers, for the kindness he'd been
    shown,
775 For the answering of his prayer. "Lord, grant me
Good lodging!" he cried, and spurring Gringolet
With his gilt heels he hurried along
The path and luckily aimed at the main
Gate and quickly came to the end

                              Of the bridge.   780
          And waited, the edge
          Of the moat in front of him, the gates
          Bolted tight, the bridge
          Up, the walls cut huge and straight.

He sat on his horse, who had halted on the bank   785
Of the deep double ditch in which
The walls were set, towering immense
Out of the water, hard stone
Hewed in the noblest style, topped
With rows of battlements, and turrets, and beautiful 790
Towers for sentries, and lovely loophole
Windows, shuttered now—he'd never
Seen a better fortress. And beyond
The walls he could see a high-roofed hall,
And pinnacled towers along it, fitted   795
To the walls, carved and crafted by ingenious
Hands. And high on those towers he saw
A host of chalk-white chimneys, gleaming
Bright in the sun—and everywhere the stone
Painted and cut, bowmen's notches   800
And watchmen's places scattered across
The castle, so it seemed scissored out of paper.
And resting on Gringolet, Gawain thought it
A pleasant place to lodge in, while the holiday
Ran—if ever he could manage to get   805
                              Inside.
          He called, and a porter
          Quickly appeared, polite,
          Standing on the wide
          Wall and greeting the knight in good order.   810

"Good sir," said Gawain, "would you carry my
    words
To the lord of this house, ask him for shelter?"
"By Peter, I can speak his heart: you're welcome
Here," said the porter, "for as long as you like."
He bowed, went down the wall and came back   815
In a moment, with men to greet Sir Gawain.
They dropped the drawbridge, came courteously out

And knelt in the snow, welcoming on their knees
That noble knight, honoring his rank;
820   They begged him to ride on that broad bridge
And he raised them with a hand and rode across.
They held his saddle, and helped him down,
And ran to stable his horse. And squires
And knights swarmed from the castle, happy
825   To escort so excellent a soldier to their hall;
When he lifted his visor they hurried to take
His helmet from his hands, anxious to serve him;
And they took his sword, and his shield. And one
By one he greeted them all, courteous,
830   And proud men pressed forward, glad at his coming.
Still in his armor they led him to the hall,
Where a huge fire crackled on the hearth.
And the lord of that company came from his
    chamber
To honor Gawain, the guest in his hall:
835   "Everything here is yours, use it
As you please; accept it as your own, for as long
                           As you like."
                And Gawain replied:
                "Thank you. May Christ
840   Reward you." And like brothers they
                    kissed
                And embraced and were glad.

And Gawain watched his gracious host
And judged him a worthy knight, tall
And strong and experienced, in the prime of life;
845   His beard was heavy, all beaver-colored,
His face as red as fire, and more fierce;
He stood firm and forbidding on thick legs;
But his words were courtly, and Gawain thought him
Worthy to lead a host of good warriors.
850   And the lord of that castle led him aside,
Commanded a man to serve him well,
And others led Gawain to a glorious bed
In a noble room, hung with strips
Of shining silk, trimmed with gold,

With a bedspread sewn in the softest fur,   855
Gleaming ermine, and around him curtains
On red-gold rings, with a rope to pull,
And silk tapestries spread on the walls
And floors, red and white silk. Then his man
Removed his armor, and his mail-shirt, pleased   860
To work with so noble a knight. And he quickly
Brought him rich robes, and Gawain
Chose which he liked, and changed his clothes,
And wore that lovely long-skirted gown—
And all at once it seemed to be Spring,   865
As his face shone, and that fair robe
Glistened with color, and Gawain walked,
Gracious, among waiting knights, and they thought,
Each of them, that Christ had made no better
                              Man.   870
            Whatever his land,
            He seemed a matchless
            Prince, meant to attack
            In the center of battle.

In front of the fireplace, where coals glowed,   875
They set him a covered chair, its cushions
Quilted and beautifully worked, embroidered
In silk; and a brown mantle, richly
Sewn, and bright, a gay cloak
Furred with the thickest skins, was thrown   880
On his shoulders; his hood, too, was ermine;
And Gawain sat in that splendid place
And soon was warm, and his spirits rose.
A long table was laid on trestles,
And a white cloth hung on it, and across it   885
Another cloth, and silver spoons,
And a salt-dish. He washed and went to his meat.
And men hurried to wait on him, brought him
Savory stews, and broths, seasoned
And hot, all double-sized portions, and fish   890
Of every kind—baked and breaded,
Grilled on charcoal, boiled, and in spiced
Soups—and sauces sweet to the tongue.

And Gawain called it a feast, graciously
895 Praised their table when they begged him to excuse it.
　　　　　　　　"This is food
　　　　　And penance together; refuse it
　　　　　If you will; tomorrow's will be better."
　　　　　He laughed and was gay, and used
900　　　　Their wine so well that he stuttered.

Then quiet questions were asked, tactful
And discreet: where had he come from, was it far?
And Gawain explained that he rode from noble
Arthur's court, that glorious king
905 Of the knights of the Round Table, and that he
Was a soldier named Gawain, sitting in their hall,
Come to their Christmas, as chance led him.
(And the lord of that castle laughed with delight,
Later, hearing that Gawain was with him.)
910 And the knights in that castle shouted with pleasure,
Proud to stand in his presence—Gawain,
Eternally praised, bearer of excellence,
Most able, most knightly, best on earth,
Most famous, most honored of men. And each of
　　them
915 Whispered to his fellow: "How sweet it will be
To see such easy, virtuous skill!
What lessons we will learn in noble speech,
What marvelous words, what practiced methods
Of converse, now that we welcome this model
920 Of perfect breeding! God has been good,
Truly, to grant us a guest like Gawain,
In this season when men sing and rejoice
　　　　　　　　In His birth.
　　　　　This knight will lead us to the meaning
925　　　　Of manners, will work
　　　　　Miracles for us to see
　　　　　In the soothing of lovers' hurts."

When dinner was done, and Gawain rose,
It was nearly night. And priests went walking
930 To their chapels, and rang out loud and merry
Chimes, as rightly they should, calling

Holiday vespers for the faithful to hear.
And the lord came, and his lady, she
In a beautiful pew, gracefully at prayer.
And Gawain hurries happily after them;   935
The lord takes him by the sleeve and leads him
To a bench, and greets him, and calls him by name,
And tells him no man could be more welcome.
And Gawain thanks him, and they throw their arms
Around each other, sit side by side   940
For the service. And the lady looked at Gawain,
And afterward, her women around her, came
To her lord, her face the fairest white,
And in all things the softest woman on earth—
Lovelier than Guenevere, in Gawain's eyes.   945
She walked round the altar, to greet him. Another
Lady led her by the left hand,
Older than her, ancient and old
And honored by a host of good knights. And how
Unlike they were, that pair, the young one   950
Fresh, the old one faded yellow;
Rich red cheeks on the one, rough
And wrinkled jowls on the other, loose
And dangling; coverings hung with pearls
On the young one's throat and breast, showing   955
Skin whiter than snow on the hillsides,
While the old one wrapped a kerchief on her neck
And hid her black chin in white
Veils and muffled her forehead in latticed
Embroidered silk, and left nothing   960
Bare but her black brows, two
Eyes, and a nose, and naked lips,
All awful to see, bleared and sour—
But a lady honored here on earth,
                                    By God!   965
            Stumpy and short,
            Her buttocks broad:
            There was better sport
            In the lady she towed.

And watching that lady watch him, Gawain   970

Went to meet them, with her lord's consent:
Bowing low, he saluted the old one,
But the pleasanter woman he wrapped in his arms
For a courteous kiss and chivalric words.
975 And the ladies asked to know him, and he quickly
Pledged himself their servant. Each lady
Took an arm, and held him, and talking as they went
They led him to a room and a fire, and called
For platters of spice-cakes, and her lord's people
980 Carried in cakes and pleasing wine.
And her lord leaped to his feet, over
And over, urging them to mirth; he tugged
At Gawain's cloak, and pulled a spear
From the wall, challenging the knight to win it
985 From him, make Christmas a merry time:
"And by my faith I'll fight to keep it,
Myself and my friends, as best I can."
And he laughed and jested, to please Sir Gawain
With jokes and games, there in his hall
990   That night,
               Until the hour
               When he called for lights,
               And they left that bower
               For sleep's delight.

995 On that morning when men remember God's birth,
His descent to earth to save our souls,
The world rejoices for His sake—and that castle
Ate and drank God's name, dishes
Of dainties and sweets on tables and at meals,
1000 Brave men celebrating in proper style:
The ancient lady at the lord's right,
And the lord come courteously to his seat beside her,
And Gawain and the gay lady together,
Between the others, when the table was laid;
1005 And the rest sitting where they thought it best.
And when everyone was seated in good order, there
     was meat
And drink and mirth, laughing and joy
So free and full that to tell it all

Would trouble my pen, however it tried.
And yet I can tell you that Gawain and the lord's   *1010*
Fair lady sat gaily side by side,
Relishing each other's laughter and courtly
Speech—private, but courteous and pure,
A surpassing sport, fit for princes
                                        And their ladies.   *1015*
            Trumpets and drums
            And pipers played;
            Each man minded his own,
            And so did the knight and the lady.

That day, and the next, were spent in delight,   *1020*
And then the third came as happily, as crowded
With joy: the Feast of St. John rang
With pleasure, and all of them thought it the end
Of their sport. And expecting to be sober, in the
    gray
Morning, they danced to the gayest music,   *1025*
And laughed, and guzzled wine. And as late
As they could, whoever had to took
Slow leave and left, finally, to stumble
Home. And saying goodnight to his host
Gawain was grasped and led to his bedroom,   *1030*
Beside the fire, an arm across
His back, and thanked for the honor he'd shown him,
Gracing his castle at that holy time,
Adorning his house. "By God, while I live,
Gawain, I'll be a better man   *1035*
For this season you've blessed." "My thanks, good
    sir,
But God almighty knows that honor
Is yours—may the Lord reward you! I sit here,
Ready and willing to do as you ask,
In anything large or small: so duty   *1040*
                                    Requires me."
            And the lord tried
            To tempt him to stay,
            And Gawain sighed,
            Knowing no way.   *1045*

Then the lord asked him about himself,
What heavy burden drove him, in those holy
Days, away from Arthur, riding
Alone in the wilderness while the world of towns
1050 Feasted. "True, true," said Gawain,
"A heavy, pressing errand takes me
To a place, somewhere, I don't know where
Or how to find it. But find it I will and
I must, by New Year's morning, with God's
1055 Help. By England, I'll find it! So let me
Ask you, sir, here and now,
If you've ever heard of a green chapel,
Anywhere in this world, and a green knight
Who holds it as his own. For he and I
1060 Have agreed to meet, made a solemn exchange
Of vows, and I'm to come there, if I can,
By New Year's morning, which is almost here.
If He would let me, I'd be happier to see
That green man—by God's own Son!—than gold
1065 Or silver or jewels. Which is why I can't stay
In your castle: I've three days' time to keep
My word; I'd rather be dead than fail."
Then the lord laughed: "Ah, now you'll stay;
I know the green chapel, forget that part
1070 Of your trouble. All in good time I'll tell you
Its place. Rest in your bed, ride
At New Year's, but not too early in the day,
And you'll be there by noon, you'll see that chapel
And that knight.
1075   Rest till the new year, friend,
        Then rise and ride
        Away. We'll set you on the right
        Road—a mile or two, then the end!"

Then Gawain was glad, and laughed: "My thanks,
1080 Host, for this above all! My adventure
Is certain: I can stay exactly as you like,
And please you in everything, perform what you
    ask."
Then the lord took him and set him at his side,

And sent for the ladies, for everyone to rejoice.
And how happy all of them were! The lord   *1085*
Babbled—all for love of Gawain—
Like a mad man never knowing what he said.
And suddenly he cried to the knight, shouting:
"Do as I ask, you'll do as I ask:
Now, will you do it now, what I ask?"   *1090*
"Sir, exactly," said the honest knight.
"Your servant for as long as I stay in your house."
"Well, you've traveled hard, and far,
Then sat up feasting with me: sleep
And rest are your needs. I know that, knight.   *1095*
So lie in your bed, high in this house,
Till mass is sung tomorrow, and eat
When you please, and with my wife: she'll keep
You company, amuse you until I make

               My way home.   *1100*

       I'll rise at dawn
       And spend the day with my hounds."
       Gawain bowed,
       Agreed, and waited. He went on:

"And more: we two can make a bargain: *1105*
Whatever I earn in the woods will be yours,
Whatever you win will be mine in exchange.
Shall we swap our day's work, Gawain? Answer
Me plain: for better or worse, an exchange?"
"By God," said Gawain, "I agree, and your pleasure *1110*
Pleases me, I like your game." "Then bring us
A pledge, and the promise is sealed," cried
The lord of that castle—and they laughed together
And drank and made delightful talk
With the ladies, for as long as they liked, and after- *1115*
    wards
Said goodnight like Frenchmen, with soft
Words and courteous speech, standing
And exchanging gracious kisses. Then they climbed
To their beds, each of them led by a crowd
Of servants holding torches high   *1120*

                   And bright.
     And still their eyes
     Met, as they climbed:
     That lord relished delight
1125   And could spin it out fine.

PART THREE

Long before dawn the castle woke:
Departing guests called for their grooms,
And men came running, saddles in hand,
And tied up their gear, and packed their bags,
And the guests came, ready to ride,   *1130*
And leaped on their horses, shook the reins,
And rode where they wanted, each to his home.
And the well-loved lord of that castle was not
The last one ready, he and his men;
After mass he ate a hasty   *1135*
Meal, and blowing his bugle galloped
To the hunt. He and his knights were set
In their saddles before the sunlight gleamed.
Huntsmen leashed up hounds, opened
Kennel doors and called out dogs,   *1140*
Blaring long notes, and loud, on their horns.
And beagles bayed and barked and snarled
And were whipped and shouted back when they
   strayed
Aside, a hundred wonderful hunters,
                              They tell me.   *1145*
            And keepers took up places
            And dogs ran free,
            And the forest swelled
            With horns and hooves and chases.

1150 At the cry of the hounds, wild animals
Shook, dazed deer in valleys
Bolted for hills—and were shut in their woods
By a shouting ring of beaters. Stags
With arching antlers were allowed through the gates,
1155 And flat-horned big bucks, for that noble lord
Had ordered that the law of the season be observed
And no man touch a male deer.
But hinds they hallooed back—"Hey hey!
Watch out!"—and they drove does deeper
1160 Into valleys, and arrows slanted down,
Great broad arrows flying at every
Turn, cutting deep in brown hides.
Hah! They screamed, and bled, and high
On slopes they died, hounds hurrying
1165 After them, and hunters with horns, blowing
So hard that the echo seemed to crack
Cliffs. And deer that escaped arrows
Were caught by keepers, cut down and killed,
Hunted back from the safety of high ground:
1170 These men all knew their trade, and their grey-
      hounds
Were so huge that leaping on a deer from behind
They tore him down, right there, as fast
                              As the telling.
            And frantic with delight
1175   The lord rode and yelled
            And ran, till night
            And darkness fell.

So the lord plays at the edge of the wood,
And Gawain lies in a lovely bed,
1180 Quiet until daylight comes creeping up the walls
And over the coverlet and around the curtains.
And sleeping in peace he heard, suddenly,
A noise at his door, and heard it swing to—
And pulling his head from the pillow he parted
1185 The edge of the curtain, and peered carefully
Out, wondering who had entered. The lady
Of that castle, beautiful to watch, silently

Shut that door behind her and approached
The bed. And Gawain, embarrassed, dropped
His head and pretended to close his eyes,   *1190*
And the lady came nearer, and quietly lifted
The curtain, and softly entered, and gently
Sat at the edge of the bed, and waited,
And watched, for Gawain to awake. And he kept
    her
Waiting, hiding his head, wondering   *1195*
Why she had come, and what she meant
To do. He thought it a strange adventure
Indeed—but said to himself, "Better
To ask, and know, than hide in sleep."
So he tossed, and stretched, and turned toward her *1200*
And opened his eyes, and played at surprise,
And crossed himself, as though to bless
                        His words.
            Her face was sweet,
            Her skin was white and pink;   *1205*
            She spoke like birds
            Singing, and her small lips laughed.

"Good morning, Gawain," said that beautiful
    woman,
"Your sleep is so innocent that anyone can catch
    you—
And now you're caught! If no one arranges   *1210*
A truce, I'll tie you to your bed—I will!"
Laughing, she teased him with a flurry of words.
"Good morning, lady," said Gawain gaily,
"Whatever you please will please your servant
Here: I surrender at once, I beg   *1215*
For mercy—the best I can hope for, now."
And he laughed with her, as they juggled words.
"My lovely captor, release me a moment,
Order me to rise and dress more properly,
So I can leave this bed, as I'd like to do.   *1220*
And a walking knight would please you more."
"Good sir," said that lovely, "stay where you are.
You're not to rise: I've better plans,

I'll lock you where you lie, and sit where I am,
1225 And then I can talk to this knight I've caught.
For I know who you are, Gawain himself,
Honored all over the world. I've heard them
Praise your perfect chivalry, pure
To lords, to ladies, to everyone alive.
1230 And here you are, and we're alone,
My lord and his men away in the woods,
All men asleep, and my maids too,
Your door shut, and locked with a bolt—
And having in my house a man so loved
1235 I refuse to waste my chance, for as long
                              As it lasts.
          Now please us both,
          Decide our path.
          Your arms are too strong,
1240   I bow to your force."

"Lord!" said Gawain. "How lucky I am,
Lady, not to be the knight you speak of:
To take that kind of honor for my own
Would be sinful; I know myself too well.
1245 By God, I'd be glad, if it pleased you, to offer you
Some different service, in word or deed:
To serve such excellence would be endless delight."
"Indeed, Sir Gawain," said that lovely lady,
"You own such excellence, such surpassing power,
1250 That to slight your ability would be lack of breeding.
How many women there are, my gentle
Knight, who'd rather hold you in their castles,
As I hold you here, and hear your courteous
Voice, and comfort their sorrows and cool
1255 Their grief, than keep their gold and treasure.
My love for our Lord who rules in Heaven
Restrains me, though His grace has given me what
    all women
                              Want."
          She spoke so well,
1260   And looked so well,

That Gawain gave her honest
Answers, free of cant.

"Madame," said that modest man, "may Mary
Reward you: your noble words, like many men's
Deeds, assign me honor and virtue   1265
That in fact I've never deserved—indeed,
When you speak such perfection, you speak of
  yourself."
"By Mary," said that wonderful woman, "no!
Even if I were worth all women
Alive, held all the wealth of the world   1270
In my hands, if I had the choice of a husband,
Ah knight, I've found you out—and now, for
Your beauty, your grace, your cheerful ways
—Exactly what I'd heard you were—nothing
And no one on earth could come before you."   1275
"Thank God!" said Gawain, "your choice was
  better.
But I'm proud to be priced so high in your eyes,
For you are my queen and I your servant
And your knight: may Christ repay you, lady."
Till the middle of the morning they spoke of many   1280
Things, the lady pretending to love him;
Gawain was cautious, walked with care
And tact.—"Were I the most beautiful on earth,"
She thought, "his heart would hang slack, thinking
                              Of the reason   1285
          For this journey, and the blow
          This season
          Will bring him." And knowing
          It was time, she took her leave.

But saying farewell, looking back   1290
With a laugh, she suddenly stunned him: "By Him
Who blesses our speech, repay me! If Gawain
Were Gawain, he'd settle his debt." "For what?"
He asked quickly, afraid that he'd failed
To frame some suitable phrase. But she smiled   1295
And wished him well: "Because," she explained,
"If Gawain were as good as his name, with every

Courtly virtue lining his heart,
He'd never have stayed so long with a lady
1300 And left her unkissed: courtesy cries out
Against him! Surely some sly word
Was missing." "Your pleasure is my command,
Lady: I kiss as you wish, as a good knight
Must. Ask me only once."
1305 She walked toward the bed, wound her arms
Around him, bent to his face, and kissed him.
With flowing words they commended each other
To Christ; she closed his door behind her,
Silent; and Gawain swiftly rose,
1310 Called to his man, chose his clothes
And was dressed, then walked happily to mass,
And then to the worthy meal that was waiting,
And then all day, till the moon shone,
                              Made merry.
1315   No better hosts sported
             With a man: every
             Moment the young lady, and the old,
             Made laughter roll.

And the lord reveled in his own pleasure,
1320 Hunting deer in meadows and woods:
Before the sun sank down he'd killed
So many no one could count them. Huntsmen
And keepers came together, proud,
And quickly collected the bodies in a pile.
1325 And the noblest knights, with their men around
       them,
Chose the sleekest deer for themselves,
Ordered them neatly quartered and carved:
(When they sliced the animals, and measured them,
       the leanest
And thinnest was two inches thick with fat).
1330 First the throat was slit, and the gullet scraped
With a sharp knife, and tied; then they cut
The legs and skinned them; then broke the belly
Open, and carefully hauled out the intestines,
Leaving the gullet knotted in place;

Then taking the throat they quickly separated   *1335*
Esophagus and windpipe, and flung out the guts;
Then carved the shoulder-bone loose, pulled it
Through a small slit, and kept the hide
Whole. Then they cut the breast in halves;
And starting to cut at the throat they ripped   *1340*
The carcass to where the front legs fork;
Emptied the edible guts; then cut
Away the membranes around the ribs:
They carved along the backbone, down
To the haunch, so the meat held together,   *1345*
Then lifted it up all at once, and cut it
At the end (properly called the numbles,
                              I know),
                    And the folds of the hind legs
                    And the meat on those bones,
                    Were quickly cut, and the spine   *1350*
                    Laid open.

Then they cut off the head, and cut off the neck,
And carved the flanks away from the spine,
And threw the ravens' fee in a thicket.   *1355*
Then they ran a hole through the ribs and hung
The carcasses by the hind legs, each
Taking the parts proper to his rank.
They set out liver and lungs and tripe
On a fresh-flayed skin, mixed with bread   *1360*
Soaked in blood, and fed their hounds.
Then hunting horns blared, and dogs bayed
As, taking their venison, hunters turned home to
High staccato bugling, loud
And clear. By sunset they had come to that castle *1365*
—And there was Gawain, quietly waiting
                              Near a bright
                    Fire, at peace.
                    The lord came to that knight,
                    Joyful, and they greeted   *1370*
                    Each other with delight.

And the lord ordered all the household
To his hall; both ladies came, with their maids;

And when everyone had gathered he commanded
    that his men
1375 Bring his venison to him; and he turned
To Gawain with a gracious laugh, asking
That he note the bushy tails of noble
Deer; and he showed the bright flesh
From their ribs. "Does it please you, this sport?
    Have I earned
1380 Your praise? Have I won appreciation with my
    skill?"
"Most certainly," said the knight. "These are the best
Game I have seen in seven winters."
"It's yours, Gawain," said the lord: "Our agreement
Lets you claim it as your own." "You are right,"
1385 Said that knight, "and I say the same, for here
In this house I have won a worthy prize,
One I am proud to make yours." He put
His arms around the lord's neck
And kissed him as courteously as a knight could:
1390 "Here are my winnings, I won no more;
I would give it gladly, were there more to give."
"I am pleased," said the lord, "and I thank you.
    Perhaps
Your winnings are the best. And perhaps you can
    tell me
Just where your skill won you this prize?"
1395 "No," said Gawain, "we said nothing of that.
You've had what I owe you: there's nothing more
                 To claim."
      They laughed, and were gay,
      And exchanged sweet words. And again
1400   They sat to supper and ate
      Famously.

And then they sat by a fire, in a private
Room, and the best of wines were brought them,
And again as they sought their beds they agreed
1405 To make the same bargain for another
Morning: whatever their winnings they'd exchange
    them

In the evening, when they met once more. Everyone
In that court heard their vows; they drank
One final toast, laughing, and took leave
Of each other, gracious to the end, and both   1410
Hurried to their beds. When the cock had crowed
And cackled for the third time, the lord
Had leaped from his blankets, and his men were
  around him.
They ate their food, and heard their mass,
And all were gone to the wood before light   1415
                              Had gleamed;
          Huntsmen and horns ran loud
          Across the fields,
          Following hounds
          Racing in the leaves.   1420

Quickly they caught a scent, along
A marsh, and the master of hounds encouraged
Their baying, shouting wild words,
And the hounds that heard him, or heard the
  barking,
Forty at once, hurried to the chase,   1425
And such a babbling uproar of dogs
Whirled up that the rocks and cliffs rang:
The huntsmen urged them on, blowing
Bugles and yelling, and they rushed along
In a pack, between a forest pool   1430
And a high cliff—and in a knoll, near the marsh,
At the foot of the cliff, with boulders tumbled
About, men and dogs stopped,
Then nosed around that knoll, in the rocks,
Until they knew he was trapped, the beast   1435
That bloodhounds had run to the ground. And they
  beat
On the bushes, and called him out, and he crashed
At a line of men, came rushing through,
The most marvelous boar, driven from his own
Herd by old age, but the hoariest,   1440
Fiercest, hugest boar in the world,
Charging out, grunting. And he drove

Three of them to the ground, and they shouted and
　　cried out,
But he ran past, quickly, not anxious
1445 To fight. "Ho! Hey! Hey!"
They hallooed, and rallied the hounds with their
　　horns.
And men and dogs lifted their voices
And ran behind him, noisily racing
　　　　　　　　　　　　　　　To a kill.
1450　　　　　And often he spun about,
　　　　　　And stood, and sliced with his snout,
　　　　　　And ripped a yelping,
　　　　　　Leaping dog, and routed

The rest. And hunters rushed as close
1455 As they dared, raining arrows on his back,
Hitting him over and over, but hurting
Nothing: the skin on his shoulders was like steel,
And no point could pierce his forehead. The smooth
Shafts shivered and broke, the metal
1460 Bounced away. And after a time
The blows began to bother him, and foaming
At the mouth he rushed at the men, and hurt them,
And many drew back in fear. Not the lord:
On a light horse he galloped behind him,
1465 Sounding his horn, calling his hunters,
Riding boldly after the boar
In the thick brushwood, till the sun sank low.
And all day long they raced through the wood,
While our gracious Gawain lay quiet and com-
　　fortable
1470 In his bed, lay easy in bright-colored blankets
　　　　　　　　　　　　　　　And sheets.
　　　　　　And the lady remembered, and came
　　　　　　To greet him
　　　　　　Early in the morning, seeking
1475　　　　　Some change in his frame

Of mind. She peered through the curtain, and
　　courteous
Gawain gave her a warm welcome,

And she gave him back as good as she got,
Sat softly at his side, laughed lightly
And said, with a cheerful glance: "Ah sir,   *1480*
Can you really be Gawain? Your soul reaches
Up for Goodness and Holiness, nothing
Else. Polite manners escape you;
Taught the truth you carefully forget it.
Yesterday I gave you instruction in the greatest   *1485*
Of love's lessons, and today it's gone."
"What lesson?" he asked. "Tell me again:
Whatever I've lost the fault must be mine."
"And yet," said that lovely, "what I taught you was
    kissing:
Whenever a lady's looks ask it,   *1490*
Claim it. That is courtesy, knight."
"Oh no," said that soldier, "you're wrong, my dear.
I cannot dare where I might be denied:
How wrong I would be to ask an unwanted
Kiss." "By our Lord," said that lord's wife,   *1495*
"You're far too strong to accept a 'no'—
If anyone were boorish enough to deny you."
"You're right!" Gawain exclaimed. "Except that
Force and threats are indecent, with friends,
And unwilling gifts are given in vain.   *1500*
My lips are yours, to kiss on command,
Lady, as long as you like, or as short:
                              Just tell me."
                    She bent to his face
                    And kissed him well,
                    Then they argued sadness and grace,   *1505*
                    Love's heavens and hells.

"Tell me, knight," said that noble lady,
"Without being angry, just why so young
And bold, so vigorous a man, so knightly,   *1510*
So courteous—and your name is known far
And wide, and a knight's good name rests
Most on his loyalty to love, his learning
In its weaponry (and stories of love's true warriors
Are title and text inscribed in their love-deeds,   *1515*

Risking their lives for a belovèd, enduring
In that great name great grief and pain,
Finally finding revenge and destroying
Sorrow, earning happiness in their true love's
1520 Arms)—just why so young and handsome
A knight, so famous in your time, could find me
Sitting at your bedside, not once but twice,
And never reveal that your head could hold
A single word of love, not one?
1525 A knight so ready with gracious vows
Should eagerly open his treasures to an innocent
Girl, teach her some signs of true love's
Skill. Hah! Is your heart unlettered,
Despite your fame? Do I seem too stupid?
1530   For shame!
                    I've come alone, tame
                    For the study of love's high game:
                    Come, while we're still alone,
                    Teach me till my husband comes home."

1535 "Christ reward you!" said Gawain. "I can't
Tell you, lady, how delighted I am
That one so noble and knowing as you
Would come here, would care to sport with so
    humble
A knight, would grant me a single warm glance.
1540 But for me to try to tell you true love's
Rules, repeat romances to you,
Knowing that you know everything I could say
And more, are wiser in love than a hundred
Like me could be if I lived to a hundred,
1545 This would make me a hundredfold fool!
As best I can, I want to obey you;
This is my duty, now and forever,
To serve you, lady, so help me God!"
And so she tested him, pushed and probed,
1550 Trying to tempt him, pretending love,
And Gawain was so gracefully evasive that he
    seemed
Always polite, and nothing happened

But happiness.
They laughed and fenced,
And at the end,   *1555*
Offering a courtly kiss,
Off she went.

And the knight rose, made ready for mass,
Then sat to a splendid dinner. He sported
With the lord's two ladies all that day,   *1560*
While the lord was racing over fields,
After the ferocious boar that rushed up
Hillsides and broke the backs of his best
Hounds, holed in till arrows drove him
On, out of shelter, to run   *1565*
In the open—arrows falling like flies
On his hide. He held them off, leaping
Wild, until at last running
Was over and, weary, he worked his way
To a rocky hole over a river.   *1570*
The hill was behind him; his hooves pawed
At the ground, foam grimaced on his snout;
And he sharpened his tusks, waiting. Tired
And still afraid, the hunters stood safely
To the side; they wanted to annoy him, but no one *1575*

Came near:
So many had been gored
By those tusks that fear
Of being torn
Held them: he seemed wild, he seemed *1580*
weird.

And then the lord rode up, urging
His horse, and saw him holed in and his hunters
Watching. He jumped lightly down, drew
His bright-polished sword and began to approach
him,
Hurrying across the ford to his hole.   *1585*
And the boar saw him, saw his bright sword,
And his hackles rose, and he snorted so loud
That the hunters were afraid for their lord's life.
Then the beast rushed out at him, straight and quick,

1590 And man and boar blended in steaming
White water; but the boar had the worst, for the lord
Had measured his charge, and aimed his sword
Into his throat, and planted it deep,
Down to the hilt, so the heart was cut,
1595 And snarling as he fell the boar surrendered
                              And dropped.
                    And a hundred hounds
                    Leaped as he stopped,
                    And hunters pulled him to the ground,
1600   And dogs bit him down.

And the horns sounded a hundred victory
Calls, and the men who still could shouted
In triumph, and the master of hounds made
His beasts bay and bark. And a hunter
1605 Trained to the art happily began
To carve that boar. He cut off the head
And planted it high on a post, then tore
Deep along the backbone, hauling
Out the intestines (broiled on coals,
1610 Dressed with bread, they were fed to the dogs).
Then he cut out the meat in gleaming slabs,
Removing the edible guts for later
Roasting, and hung the two halves together
And roped them to a heavy rod. Then they hurried
1615 Home, carrying the carcass; the head
Was paraded in front of the lord himself,
Who had battled the boar to death with his own
                              Strong hands.
                    The trek to his hall
1620   And Gawain seemed longer than all
                    The long hunt. He came, he called,
                    And there Gawain stands.

Laughing loud, shouting a merry
Speech, the lord exulted, seeing
1625 Gawain. His ladies came, and the court,
And he showed them the thick flesh, told them
How huge a beast he had fought, how fierce

When they'd finally cornered him deep in the
   forest.
And Gawain gave him the praise he deserved,
Told him how well he'd proved his worth;   *1630*
So immense a beast, such massive slabs
Of meat, he'd never seen before.
They hefted that huge head, and Gawain
Admired it, and admired the lord's fierce courage
In cutting it off. "Now Gawain, it's yours;   *1635*
We've agreed, you know our game. That's settled."
"I know," said the knight, "and just as truly
Let me give you, once more, everything I got
For myself." He embraced the lord, and kissed him,
And immediately kissed him again. "We are quit," *1640*
Said Gawain, "here, tonight, as we agreed
To be; the bond has been kept, to the letter
                     And complete."
         "Ah by Saint Giles," swore the lord,
         "I can't compete: *1645*
         There's nothing you won't afford
         If you always trade so sweet."

They set up tables on trestles, covered them
With cloth, and kindled a clear bright light
With waxed torches, mounted on walls;   *1650*
Men rushed about with platters and meat;
And around the blazing fire they laughed
And were happy, singing (both at supper
And after) a host of beautiful songs,
Christmas part-songs, and untried carols,   *1655*
As merry as a man can tell of, and always
The lord's lady was seated beside
Gawain. And so loving were her glances, her speech,
Her winks, her secret marks of favor,
That the knight was stunned, and angry with himself, *1660*
But courtesy kept him civil, he made himself
Gracious and kind, no matter how twisted
                    Things turned.
        And when food and laughter
        Had ended together,   *1665*

> They gathered where a fire burned
> In a private chamber,

And chatted and drank, and wondered whether
To make the same agreement for New Year's
1670 Eve, and Gawain asked to leave
In the morning, arguing that his time had almost
Come. But the lord argued against it:
"As I am a knight, I give you my word,
Gawain, that you'll get to that green chapel
1675 And your errand there, early on New Year's
Day. You rest high in your room,
I'll hunt in the forest, and we'll hold our agreement
As it was, trading profit for profit,
For I've tested you twice, and you've proved your-
      self true.
1680 The third throw will come up best, cast
The die, drink while we can, and rejoice,
For sorrow we can have whenever we seek it."
And Gawain agreed, and agreed to stay,
And they drank it in wine, then walked behind
      torches
1685   To their beds.

> Gawain slept
> Peaceful and quiet;
> But the lord dressed
> Early, he had tricks to try.

1690 He and his men heard mass, gulped
A morsel, then sought their horses in that sweet
Morning air. All of his huntsmen
Sat ready mounted, in front of the hall.
The world was beautiful, hung with frost,
1695 And the huge red sun rose through clouds
And came, white and gleaming, to the sky.
Beside a wood they unleashed their hounds,
And rocky hillsides rang with their horns:
The fox's trail was found, they followed it
1700 Close to the ground, keeping it warm;
A beagle bayed, the huntsman hallooed him,
And the rest of the dogs rushed where he'd called,

A snorting pack running in the fox's
Footsteps, as he ran in front of them; they found
   him,
Saw him, and ran as fast as they could,   *1705*
Crying his fate with fierce yelps,
While he dodged and doubled about in bushes
And thorns, stopping by hedges to listen.
And then he leaped a fence, by a little
Ditch, and crawled across a bit   *1710*
Of marsh, hoping the hounds would miss him,
And suddenly, before he could stop, he found
That three of the snarling greyhounds had leaped
                       For his throat.
       He swerved in his tracks,   *1715*
       Ran swiftly back
       Where he'd come; loaded
       With grief he raced to the wood.

How good it was to hear those greyhounds,
Gathered around him, ringing him in: *1720*
The curses they called on his head clattered
As if the cliffs had fallen. A man
Would find him, and shout, and snarling tongues
Would follow his feet across the forest.
They labeled him "thief," threatened his life,   *1725*
And he could not hesitate, the hounds ran fast:
If he left the wood they were waiting, but he knew
How to hide and ran in, swift and clever.
And in fact he led them by the heels, the lord
And his men, past midday, dodging in the hills,   *1730*
While gracious Gawain slept at peace
In those noble curtains, on that cold morning.
But the lady—for love!—refused herself sleep.
Not expecting to fail, her purpose firm,
She rose from her bed, and quickly went to him,   *1735*
Wrapped to her feet in a gay mantle
Furred with perfect blended skins,
And her hair held in a jeweled net
Set with stones by the dozen; her beautiful
Face and her throat were carefully bare,   *1740*

Her dress cut low in front and in back.
She came to his room, closed his door
Behind her, opened a window and called him
Awake, laughing and scolding with cheerful

1745   Words:
        "Oh! How can you sleep
        When the morning's so clear?" He was
           deep
        In a miserable dream
        But that speech he heard.

1750 He'd been mumbling and tossing, lost in his night-
      mare
Like a man deeply troubled in mind,
Remembering how fate was scheduled to come to
      him
Tomorrow, at the green chapel, with the green man's
Stroke, and he could not fight: he recovered
1755 His wits, hearing the lady's words,
And struggled awake, answering quickly.
And she came to the bed, laughing sweet,
And bent to his face, and gave him a graceful
Kiss; he composed his face, and welcomed her
1760 Warmly. And seeing how beautiful she was,
And how dressed, and her face, and her body, and
      her flesh
So white, joy welled in his heart.
With gentle smiles they started to talk,
And their talk was of joyful things, they spoke only
1765   Of bliss.
        Words came flowing free,
        Each was pleased
        With the other; and only Mary
        Could save him from this.

1770 That beautiful princess pressed him so hard,
Urged him so near to the limit, he needed
Either to take her love or boorishly
Turn her away. To offend like a boor
Was bad enough; to fall into sin
1775 Would be worse, betraying the lord of that house.

"God willing," he thought, "it will not happen!"
He parried, with a loving laugh, her passionate
Speeches, her talk of special favor.
She told him: "Shame is all you deserve,
Refusing to love a lady who lies   1780
Beside you, her heart weeping openly,
Unless there's a lover your heart likes better,
To whom your faith's so firmly tied
That nothing can loosen it. And now I know,
And pray you, sir, to tell me truly: 1785
Love's not love that hides the truth
                    From love."
        He said: "By good Saint John,"
        And smiled to prove
        His claim, "I've none,   1790
        And none will have for now."

"And those," she exclaimed, "are the ugliest words
In the world! You've told me the truth, and hurt me
Hard. Kiss me, and I'll leave you here
Alone. I'm a woman with sorrow, not love."   1795
Sighing, she stooped and quietly kissed him,
Then left his side, saying: "Now dear,
Here at this parting grant me this,
Give me something, your glove, some gift
Of your own, to remember you with, to soften   1800
My sorrow." "By God," said Gawain, "I wish
The daintiest thing in the world were here
In my hand, to match my devotion; but you're
   worthy
Of more, lady, than I'm able to give you.
Some trifle, some worthless token, is infinitely   1805
Less than your honor deserves—a simple
Glove is no keepsake I could bear to give you.
I'm empty-handed, here, alone
On a pilgrimage to an unknown land; I've no porters
With gifts. It wears at my heart, lovely,   1810
Not to oblige you, but a man must do
                  As he must.
        Do not resent it, sweet."

"Never," said that lusty
1815 Lady. "But see:
If I've nothing from you, you'll have this
from me."

She offered a red gold ring, richly
Worked, set with a dazzling stone
That shone like the sun—a gift suitable
1820 For the ransoming of kings. But Gawain refused it,
Saying at once: "My lady fair,
In God's own name there's nothing I can take,
Not now, when I've nothing to give in return."
She offered it again; he declined, gently
1825 Vowing he could never accept. And that noble
Woman, pained, tried once more:
"If my ring is really too rich a gift,
Then be less in my debt, but take my belt,
Neither as costly nor as good." She quickly
1830 Drew it from around her waist, knotted
Over her tunic, under her cloak:
Trimmed with gold, it was green silk
Embroidered with stones, but only at the edges.
And she held it in her hand, begged that he take it,
1835 Worthless, unworthy as it was. He refused,
Explaining that until, by the grace of God,
He was able to end the adventure he'd begun,
He could never touch either gold or treasure.
"And I beg you, lady, not to be angry,
1840 And to give this over, for I cannot and I will not
Agree.
For your kindness I owe you
A knight's fealty,
And I'll always show you
1845 The service I know you

Deserve." "You refuse this silk," she said,
"Which seems such a trifle? So it may seem.
See how small it is! And how slight.
But whoever knows what's woven in its threads
1850 Would value it rather more, I suppose:

For any man bound with this belt,
This green lace locked around him,
Can never be killed, here under God's
Own heaven—no blow, no trick, nothing
Can hurt him." Gawain hesitated, his heart   1855
Reached for protection, like a thief for a gem:
He could come to that chapel, and take that stroke,
And with this glorious device walk off
Unharmed. He held his tongue, allowed her
To speak—and she pressed it on him, urgent—   1860
And he was ready to surrender, then smiling,
   surrendered,
And agreed, as she asked, to stay silent, to hide
The gift from her husband, agreed that only
She and Gawain would share the secret
                    Forever.   1865
        And he thanked her, happy
        And gracious as never
        Before. And she tapped
        Three kisses to his cheek all together.

Then she took her leave, and left him there;   1870
Her games with Gawain were over. And after
She'd gone that knight quickly got himself
Up out of bed and properly dressed,
And he hid her love-gift in a safe place,
Covering it carefully so he could find it later.   1875
Then he went swiftly to the chapel, walked
Inside and sought a priest in private,
Asked to have his confession heard,
His soul instructed in the pathways to heaven.
And he told his sins, small and large,   1880
And prayed for the mercy of almighty God,
And begged the priest to absolve him, and his soul
Was anointed so completely clean that the Day
Of Judgment could have come with the sun, and
   been welcome.
And he pleased himself with the lord's two ladies,   1885
Singing carols and making merry

As never before in that house, until night
> Fell.
>> And all the lord's men
1890 >> Were pleased: "How easy to tell
>> That he's happy again
>> At last, and we've treated him well."

Now leave him in that comfort, where love had
   come to him!
The lord is still in the fields, hunting
1895 His pleasure. The fox is finally at bay:
Leaping a fence, the lord spied him
Cutting across a thick grove,
The sound of hounds hurrying him along
And behind him the pack, yelping at his heels.
1900 Seeing him come, the lord waited,
Drew his sword and swung it. And the fox
Swerved, and as he swerved pulled back,
But a hound had him before he was free,
And in front of the horses' hooves they fell on him,
1905 And the barking grew fierce as they bit him to death.
The lord dismounted, quickly lifted him
Over his head, shouting to the hunters,
While the hounds leaped and bayed like wolves,
Slobbering with desire for meat. And his men
1910 Ran up, sounding their horns, signaling
Hunters to come where the beast had been caught.
And after everyone had come, whoever
Bore a bugle blew it, and whoever
Had no horn hallooed, and with hounds
1915 Baying the merriest music on earth
They roared a royal flourish for Renard's
> Soul.
>> They stroked and rubbed their dogs,
>> And rewarded them all,
1920 >> Then keeping the fur whole
>> They stripped it off.

Then they turned home, in the twilight glow,
Sounding their horns as they rode. And at last
The lord arrived at his belovèd home,

Where a fire was burning, and Gawain was seated 1925
Beside it, waiting, smiling and at ease,
Happy at the sport he'd had with the ladies:
His rich blue mantle reached to the ground,
His jacket was lined with lovely soft fur,
Like the hood that hung across his shoulders, 1930
Both of them bright with ermine. And Gawain
Met the lord in the middle of his hall,
With his men around him, and greeted him gra-
      ciously.
"First let me keep our agreement, made
Last night and sealed in such flowing wine." 1935
He threw his arms around his host
And kissed him three times, three vigorous kisses.
"By Christ," said the lord, "getting these goods
Must be merry hunting, if the price is right."
"Who cares about cost?" said Gawain quickly. 1940
"What I've owed you I've paid you, here in the
      open."
"And I," the lord replied, "pay you
Less, for in all this long day's hunting
This miserable fox skin's my prize—may the devil
Earn as much!—and three such kisses 1945
As you gave me are better than a dozen bedraggled
                        Hides."
            "Enough," said Gawain, "by God
            I thank you for the fruit of your ride."
            And the hunt, and the hard 1950
            Chase were described.

And they sang and were sung to, and ate as they
      liked—
The lord and Gawain drank to the ladies,
And the ladies laughed, and jests were exchanged—
Enjoying themselves as much as men can 1955
Except in halls neither sane nor sober.
Everyone joked, knights and nobles
And their lord, till the time for parting, and they
      finally
Rose and made their way to bed.

1960 And Gawain took humble leave of the lord,
     A courtly farewell of grateful words:
     "For this marvelous visit I've had in your house,
     Your Christmas grace to me, may God repay you!
     Enroll me forever as one of your knights.
1965 Tomorrow, as you know, I must ride on my way:
     Assign me, please, the guide you promised,
     To show me that green chapel, where God
     Has decreed that on New Year's Day I must meet
     My fate." "By my faith," swore the lord, "you'll find me
1970 Ready to give you everything I agreed to."
     And he chose a servant to set him on the road,
     Lead him through hills as quickly as could be,
     Guide him on good paths across
                           Woodlands.
1975   And Gawain thanked him, and kissed
          His hands,
          Then turned to the two grand
          Ladies, and wished them

     Farewell, sadly exchanging kisses,
1980 Urging his gratitude with polished grace—
     Which the ladies returned as good as they got,
     With sorrowful sighs commending him to Christ.
     And courteous to all, he left them all,
     Thanking every man he met
1985 For his kindness, the particular pains he'd taken,
     Serving Gawain as his lord's guest.
     And every man regretted his going,
     Almost convinced they'd relished his honor
     All their lives. Then they led him to his room
1990 And brought him to his bed, where rest waited.
     But whether he slept or not I dare not
     Say; he could have remembered many
                            Things.
          Yet let him lie as he will,
1995   His adventure ringing
          In his ears. Sit still
          A moment more, and I'll sing it.

PART FOUR

Now New Year's comes, and the night passes,
Daylight replaces darkness, as God
Decrees. But storms crackled through the world, *2000*
Clouds tumbled their bitter cold
On the earth, northwinds freezing the poor;
Snow shivered in the air, and animals
Shook; the wind whistled from the hills
And drove snowdrifts down in the valleys. *2005*
And Gawain listened, lying in his bed;
His eyelids were closed, but he slept little.
Each cockcrow told him what hour had come.
And just before dawn he rose, dressing
Quickly by the light of a lamp; then he called *2010*
His groom, who came running, and ordered him
To bring his mail-shirt and Gringolet's saddle.
His weapons and all his armor were brought,
And Gawain was made magnificently ready:
First wool, against the winter cold, *2015*
And then his brightly polished war-gear,
The belly shield, and the steel plates,
And the gleaming rings of his mail-shirt, all ready,
Shining as when he'd worn them to that castle.
                                        His groom *2020*
               Had wiped and rubbed them
               Inch by inch. No man

Was handsomer from Rome
To Dublin.

2025 And though he wore the most glorious clothes
—A heraldic vest embroidered over
In velvet, with magical jewels mounted
In front, and seams sewn in color,
All lined inside with the softest fur—
2030 He also wore the lady's gift,
Well aware of his own best interest:
When his sword hung at his side, he wound
That belt twice around him, wrapped it
Quickly, happily across his waist,
2035 The bright green silk shining beautifully
Against the royal red of his tunic.
But Gawain was indifferent to that rich glow,
To the polished stones gleaming at its fringe,
To the gold glittering at either end,
2040 Determined to save his neck when he bent it
Toward death, tamely taking an axe-blow,
                              A knife-stroke.

            Dressed,
            Armed, he left
2045   The castle, quickly walked
            To his horse, thanking the noble folk

Around him. And Gringolet was ready, stood huge,
Waiting, well-fed, well-lodged, when his master
Rested, now strong and ready to gallop.
2050 And seeing his sleek flanks, Gawain
Quietly exclaimed, his words sober:
"There are men, in this castle, who care about
    courtesy,
And their lord maintains them—may they live in
    joy!
May love be his lovely lady's reward!
2055 When they open these gates, when they welcome a
    guest,
Honor flows from their hands! May the Lord
Of us all reward them, who rules in Heaven.
And if I survive, here on earth,

May I live to reward you myself!" Then he set
His foot in the stirrups and swept to the saddle;   *2060*
His shield was brought, and he took it on his
    shoulder,
And with golden heels he spurred Gringolet,
And he stopped prancing, leaped forward
                    On the pavement;
        His rider was mounted,   *2065*
        Spear and sword waved
        In the air. "May Christ save
        This castle," Gawain pronounced.

Then the drawbridge came down, and the thick
    gates
Drew back, swung open, unbarred. And the knight   *2070*
Crossed himself and rode across;
He blessed the porter, who kneeled before him,
Wished him Godspeed and God's good will
For Gawain; then almost alone, rode off,
Following in his guide's footsteps, leading him   *2075*
Along the dangerous road to that axe-
Stroke. Trees stood bare, on the slopes
Where they rode, and the rocky cliffs lay frozen.
Clouds blew high, but the sky was ugly;
Mist drizzled, melted on the mountains,   *2080*
Every hill wore a hat, a cloak
Of fog. Brooks foamed at their banks,
Splashing on the shore, bright, where they flowed.
Their path wound wild, around a wood,
Till the time when the winter sun rises   *2085*
                    In the sky:
        Snow covered the high
        Hill they rode on, white
        And cold; and the guide
        Drew up, asked Gawain to halt.   *2090*

"I've brought you this far; now you've come close,
Knight, to that place you've been hunting, scurrying
And prying so hard to find. Let
Me speak to you privately, for I know who you are,

2095 And I speak as someone who loves you: if you'll
     listen
     To me, you'll manage this business better.
     That place where you're hurrying is dangerous,
     knight:
     The most horrible creature in the world lives
     In that wilderness, a grim wildman who loves
2100 To kill, the hugest creature on the earth,
     Bigger and stronger than four of Arthur's
     Best knights, or Hector, or anyone else.
     He waits in that green chapel, grim,
     Determined, and no one rides by, no knight
2105 Proud of his sword, but he beats him to death
     With one blow. A ruthless man, born
     Pitiless, who kills priests or peasants,
     Monks or abbots, anyone who passes:
     Killing is as natural as air, to him!
2110 And so I say to you, sitting in your saddle,
     If you go there, you're dead: it's the simple truth,
     Knight—dead if you'd twenty lives
                                    To lose!
              He's lived there for years,
2115   He kills as he chooses:
              Fight without fear,
              Gawain, but you're bound to lose.

     "And so, good sir, leave him in peace,
     In the name of God pick some different
2120 Path! Ride wherever Christ takes you,
     And I'll hurry home, and I promise you, knight,
     I swear by God and all His saints,
     I'll swear by any oath you ask,
     That I'll keep your secret, conceal this story
2125 Forever, keep it from everyone on earth."
     "By God," said Gawain, grimly polite,
     "I'm grateful, fellow, for all your good wishes;
     I believe you'd keep it secret, I believe you.
     But however loyally you lied, if I rode
2130 Away, fled for fear, as you tell me,
     I'd be a coward no knight could excuse.

Whatever comes, I'm going to that chapel,
And I'll meet that wild man: however it happens
It will happen, for evil or good, as fate
                              Decides;   2135
                    However wild
                    He may be,
                    God can see,
                    God can save."

"By Mary!" said the man, "you've said so much   2140
Of your bravery that the blame will be yours when
   you lose
Your life. You want to lose it: proceed.
Your helmet's on your head, your spear's in your
   hand:
Ride along the rocky side
Of this path; you'll come to a wild valley;   2145
On your left, a little farther down,
You'll see exactly what you want, that green
Chapel, and the green oaf who owns it.
Gawain the noble, go in God's name!
I wouldn't join you for all the gold   2150
In the world, not a foot further through this wood."
And he swung his horse around, dug
His heels in its side, and raced away,
Leaving Gawain with no guide, alone
                              In that wood.   2155
                    "God is good,"
                    Said the knight. "I'll not weep
                    Or complain: I keep
                    My trust in Him, I'll do as He would."

Then he spurred Gringolet down the path,   2160
Across a slope, beside a grove,
Riding a rough road to the valley
Below. Then he looked about. It seemed wild,
No sign of shelter anywhere, nothing
But steep hills on every side,   2165
Gnarled crags with huge rocks,
Crags scratching at the sky! He stopped,

Pulled back on the reins, held Gringolet ready
While he stared this way and that, seeking
2170 The chapel. He saw nothing—except
A queer kind of mound, in a glade
Close by, a rounded knoll near a stream,
Set right on the bank, beside the brook:
And that water bubbled as though it were boiling!
2175 He sent Gringolet forward, stopped
Near the mound, dismounted and tied his horse
To a lime-tree, looping the reins on a branch.
Then he walked closer, walked around
The knoll, trying to think what it was.
2180 He saw holes at the end and the sides,
Saw patches of grass growing everywhere,
And only an old cave inside—
A hole—a crevice in a crag: he couldn't
      Tell.
2185   "My Lord, my Lord," said that courteous knight,
  "Can this be the chapel? At midnight,
  Here, the devils of hell
  Could pray their prayers quite well!

  "By Jesus, it's lonely here: this chapel
2190 Is ugly, gruesome, all overgrown.
But a good place for the green knight,
He could serve the devil properly, here.
By Christ, it's Satan who struck me with this
  meeting,
I feel it! He's sent me here to destroy me.
2195 What an evil church: may destruction end it!
The most cursèd chapel I've ever come to!"
His helmet on his head, spear in his hand,
He climbed across to its rough roof—
Then heard, from a high hill, on a boulder,
2200 Beyond the brook, a violent noise—
What! It clattered on the cliff, as if
To split it, like a grindstone grinding a scythe.
What! It whirred like water at a mill.
What! It rushed and it rang, and it sang
2205 Miserably. "That's meant for me," said Gawain,

"A kind of greeting. By Christ, I'll greet him
                              Better.
               God's will be done!—'Alas, alas!'—
               What good is wailing? It never
               Helps; I'll never gasp,   2210
               Though my life be severed."

Then he raised his voice, calling out loud:
"Who lives in this place? who's here as he promised
To be? Gawain is walking right
On your roof. If you want him, come to him quickly, 2215
Now or never, let's have it done with."
"Just wait," said someone up over his head,
"What you're waiting to have, you'll have in a
    hurry."
But he stayed where he was, working that wheel
With a whirring roar. Then he stopped, and stepped 2220
Down across a crag, came
Through a hole, whirling a fierce weapon,
A long-bladed battle-axe, sharpened for the stroke,
Its massive blade bent to the shaft,
Filed like a knife, on a grindstone four feet   2225
Wide; a leather strap hung at
Its length; and the green man looked as he'd looked
At the start, his skin and his beard and his face,
Except that he skipped like a dancer, setting
His axe-handle on stones and leaping along.   2230
At the brook, to keep dry, he leaned on the handle
And hopped across, and hurried to Gawain,
Grim on a broad battlefield covered
                              With snow.
               And Gawain waited,   2235
               Not bowing low;
               And the green man said: "You came:
               I can trust you now.

"Be careful, Gawain! You're welcome," the green
    man
Went on, "here in my home, you've made   2240
A difficult journey, and you came on time,
You've kept your faith. Now keep the rest:

A year ago I gave you your chance;
Today the turn is mine. We're completely
2245 Alone, in this valley; no one can come
Between us, however fiercely we fight.
Take off your helmet, and take my axe-stroke.
Hold yourself still, as I did when you slashed
My head from my shoulders with a single blow."
2250 "By God," said Gawain, "may the Holy Ghost
Grant me the power to begrudge you nothing.
Keep to the bargain, swing just once,
And I'll stand still, and you'll do exactly
                                        As you please."

2255   And he bent his neck, leaned
       Forward; the white flesh gleamed.
       He tried to seem
       Fearless, but his knees

Were weak. And the green man got ready, lifted
2260 That huge axe in both his hands,
Swung it up with all his strength,
And pretended to swing straight at his neck.
If he'd hurled it down as he swung it high
Gawain would have been dead forever.
2265 But the knight looked to the side, and saw it
Coming, glittering as it fell to his throat,
And he pulled his shoulders back, just a bit,
And the green man jerked the blade away,
And poured a host of proud words on that prince:
2270 "Gawain? You can't be Gawain, his name
Is too noble, he's never afraid, nowhere
On earth—and you, you flinch in advance!
I've heard nothing about Gawain the coward.
And I, did I flinch, fellow, when you swung
2275 At my neck? I never spoke a word.
My head fell, and I never flinched.
And you, before it can happen your heart
Is quaking. Who doubts that I'm the better
                                        Man?"
2280   "I flinched," said Gawain,
       "I won't again.

And this much is plain:
My head, if it falls, won't talk in my hands.

"But get it done, let it be over.
Bring me my fate, and bring it quickly.   2285
I'll stand like a stone: on my word of honor
My neck will be still till your stroke comes to it."
"Have at you, then!" he cried, and heaved it
Up, and glared as fierce as a madman.
He swung it sharply, but not at his neck,   2290
Held it back, before it could hurt him.
And Gawain waited, stood like a stone,
Or the stump of a tree tied to the ground
By a hundred tangled roots. And the green man
Laughed and told him, gaily: "I take it   2295
You're ready, now, and it's time to strike.
Let Arthur's knighthood save your neck,
That noble rank protect you, if it can."
And Gawain replied, angry and ashamed:
"May the better man strike. You talk too long: 2300
Perhaps you've frightened yourself with these
    threats?"
"Ah well," said the green man, "you've turned so
    brave
That I need to delay no longer. Your time
                        Is now."
                        He took up a stance,   2305
                        And his face scowled,
                        And to Gawain his chances
                        Of living seemed scant.

He swung his weapon swiftly up,
And down, the blade toward the bare flesh;   2310
And he struck hard, but hurt him only
With a nick, that snipped the skin. The edge
Grazed Gawain's white neck, and bright
Blood shot from his shoulder to the ground,
And as soon as he saw that gleam on the snow   2315
He leaped forward a spear-length or more,
Throwing his helmet furiously into place,
Jerking his shield around in front of him,

Drawing his sword, and speaking fiercely—
2320 Never since his mother bore him had he known
Half the happiness he suddenly felt:
"Stop, green man! Don't swing again!
I've taken a single stroke, and stood still for it:
No more, or else I'll repay you in kind—
2325 Believe me, fellow, I'll pay you fully
                    And well.
        You've had your stroke,
        And one was all
        We agreed to, in Arthur's hall.
2330   And so, sir, stop, halt!"

The green man stood listening, leaning on his axe
(It was upside down, he rested on the blade),
And watching the knight, how bravely he waited,
How unafraid, armed and ready,
2335 Standing alert. And he liked what he saw.
And then he spoke, with a cheerful, booming
Voice, addressing Gawain: "Warrior,
Soldier, no need to be fierce, now.
No one's used you badly, shown you
2340 Discourtesy; what was done was what we agreed.
I owed you a stroke, I've paid you a stroke:
I release you from any and all obligations.
Perhaps, if my hands were quicker, I could have
Dealt you a better blow, and done harm.
2345 I pretended one stroke, a threat, a joke,
But left you whole; I had the right,
Because of our other agreement, in my castle;
You kept it faithfully, performed like an honest
Man, gave me everything you got.
2350 Except that you kissed my wife: I swung
For that reason—but you gave me back her kisses.
So all you got, for that, was a puff
                    Of air:
        An honest man
2355   Need never fear.
        But still, the third day, there

In my castle, you failed—and you felt
    that, here.

"That belt you're wearing: it's mine, my wife
Gave it to you—I know it all, knight,
The kisses you took, and gave, and all   2360
You did, and how she tempted you: everything.
For I planned it all, to test you—and truly,
Not many better men have walked
This earth, been worth as much—like a pearl
To a pea, compared to other knights.   2365
But you failed a little, lost good faith—
Not for a beautiful belt, or in lust,
But for love of your life. I can hardly blame you."
And Gawain stood silent, stood a long time,
So burdened with grief that his heart shuddered: 2370
His blood ran like fire in his face,
He winced for shame at the green man's words.
And finally he found words of his own:
"A curse on cowardice and a curse on greed!
They shatter chivalry, their vice destroys   2375
Virtue." Then he loosened the belt, unfastened it,
And grimly threw it to the green man. "There!
Take the faithless thing, may it rot!
Fear of your blow taught me cowardice,
Brought me to greed, took me from myself   2380
And the goodness, the faith, that belong to knight-
    hood.
I'm false, now, forever afraid
Of bad faith and treachery: may trouble, may
    sorrow

                    Come to them!
          Oh knight: I humbly confess   2385
          My faults: bless me
          With the chance to atone.
          I'll try to sin less."

Then the green man laughed, and courteously ex-
    plained:
"The damage you did me is cured, it's gone.   2390
You stand confessed so clean, you took

Such plain penance at the point of my axe,
That I hold you cleansed, as pure in heart
As if from your birth to this day you'd never
2395 Sinned! And Gawain, I give you this belt,
As green as my gown. Remember your challenge,
Here, as you walk your way among knights
And princes, keep this token for chivalrous
Men to know your adventure at the green
2400 Chapel. And now, in this New Year, come
To my castle again, and we'll finish this festival
                                With good cheer."
         And he pressed him to come,
         Saying, "My wife will be there,
2405   You can make her your friend, who was once
         Your bitter foe."

"No, truly," said Gawain, taking
Off his helmet, and thanking the green knight
Courteously. "I've lingered long enough.
2410 May happiness come to you, from Him who decrees
All honors! And convey my wishes to your gracious
Wife, and that other honored lady,
Who cleverly tricked their knight. No wonder:
There's nothing remarkable in their making a man
2415 Foolish, in women winning men
To sin, for Adam our father was deceived
Just so, and Solomon, and also Samson—
Delilah was his death—and later David
Endured misery for Bathsheba's beauty.
2420 Women ruined them: how wonderful if men
Could love them well, but never believe them!
And these were the noblest knights of their time,
The best, the very best, who walked
                         The world
2425   In those days—and women tied them
         In knots, whirled them
         In circles. I've been beguiled,
         As they were: this excuse should be heard.

"But your belt," said Gawain, "may God reward
you!

I'll keep it, gladly, not for its gold,   2430
Nor its lovely silk, nor its polished stones,
Not its cost, nor for honor, nor the glorious craft
That made it, but to see it, often, as a sign
Of my sin: if I ride in glory, to remember
The weakness and error of this feeble flesh,   2435
How easily infected with the filth of sin—
And if ever pride for my feats of arms
Stirs me, this belt will humble my heart.
One thing let me ask you, without offense:
You rule that land where I lived, where I rested   2440
In your castle—may He repay you who keeps
The stars in the sky and sits in Heaven!—
Tell me only your name, nothing
More." "Gladly," said the green knight. "I am
Bercilak de Hautdesert. Morgana   2445
Le Fay, who lives in my house, a famous
Witch, with wonderful magic learned
From Merlin, the master of that art—for she shared
His bed, once, that noble wizard
And wise man, who knows the knights of Arthur's   2450
                         Hall:
              Morgana the goddess she's called,
              And no one in all
              The world could resist her call
              If she bade him come—   2455

Morgana sent me to your king's castle,
To test your pride, to determine the truth
Of the Round Table's fame, and the tales that tell it.
She hoped my lopped-off head would addle
Your brains, would frighten Arthur's queen   2460
And kill her with fear, a green ghost
Standing at her table, speaking, head
In hand. And that ancient lady, Morgana,
Is also Arthur's half-sister, your aunt,
Daughter of the Duchess of Cornwall—that Duchess 2465
By whom Uther Pendragon had Arthur.
And again I ask you to come to your aunt,
Be merry in my house; my men love you,

And I want you there, by my faith, for myself,
2470 As much as I've ever wanted anyone."
And Gawain again said no, he could not.
They embraced, and kissed, and commended each
  other
To Christ, and parted, there on that snow-covered
                                         Field;
2475   And Gawain and Gringolet rode home
                  To Arthur's castle, and the green
                  Knight rode where he pleased,
                  Alone.

Now Gawain rides in the world's wilderness,
2480 Alive by the gracious mercy of God.
He slept under roofs, he slept under trees,
And he knew adventures, and won victories,
That I hope to tell some different time.
The nick in his neck had grown whole;
2485 He wore that gleaming belt slanted
Across his tunic, tied beneath
His arm, as a sign and token of the sin
He'd committed, and his sorrow and shame. And so
He arrived at court, safe and sound.
2490 And the king, when he heard, called to his knights,
Laughing, delighted, that Gawain was home.
And he kissed his knight, and the queen kissed him,
And a host of noble soldiers greeted him,
Asked his adventures; and he told them marvelous
2495 Things, never concealing his hardships,
Told them of the chapel, described the green
  knight,
Talked of the lady, and at last of the belt.
He showed them the faint scar on his neck,
Sign of his treachery, given as a loving
2500   Warning.
                  He groaned, admitting it,
                  Suffered torment;
                  Blood flooded the skin
                  In his face, as he mourned it.

2505 "My lord," said Gawain, lifting the belt,

"This band and the nick on my neck are one
And the same, the blame and the loss I suffered
For the cowardice, the greed, that came to my soul.
This sign of bad faith is the mark of my sin:
I'll wear it on my waist as long as I live,   *2510*
For a man may hide an injury to his soul,
But he'll never be rid of it, it's fastened forever."
The king consoled him, and all that court,
And they laughed and resolved, then and there,
That lords and ladies of Arthur's Table   *2515*
Would each of them wear a slanted belt
Around their waists, woven of green,
To keep company with their well-loved Gawain.
And that belt was the glory of Arthur's Round
    Table;
Its knights wore it forever more,   *2520*
As the best books of romances tell.
And so in Arthur's time this adventure
Took place, as the Book of Brutus bears witness,
After that bold Brutus appeared
In Britain, when the siege and assault had done   *2525*
                    For Troy;
            And other adventures as well,
            Of great and loyal
            Knights. Now may the royal
            King of the world keep us from Hell!   *2530*

H O N Y S O Y T Q U I M A L P E N C E
        [Shame to him who finds evil here]

AFTERWORD

þer is no haþel vnder heuen tohewe hym þat my3t
(Lines 1854–1855)
"*. . . no blow, no trick, nothing/Can hurt him*"

þer hade ben ded of his dynt þat do3ty watz euer
(Line 2264)
"Gawain would have been dead forever"

Withhelde heterly his honde, er hit hurt my3t
(Line 2291)
"Held it back, before it could hurt him"

These three passages from Sir *Gawain and the Green
Knight* (the Middle English from the Tolkien/Gordon/
Davis edition, hereafter called TGD; the translation
by Burton Raffel) refer to the "magic" girdle and then
to its "effectiveness" against the Green Knight's axe-
blows. They are, clearly, contradictory: either the lace
will protect Gawain or it will not. Contradiction can
suggest such critical terms as tension, dialectic, para-
dox, ambiguity, and irony. These are terms primarily
descriptive of structure or technique (in the sense of
trope or device). Yet in context, that is, employing the
evidence of the poem as a whole, it should be equally
clear that there is no contradiction. The girdle is no
more magic than the lady's love for Gawain is real.
The Green Knight could just as easily sever the hero's
head as nick his neck. We believe what the poet says

in lines 2264 and 2291, but we have every reason to doubt what the lady says in lines 1854–1855.

The apparent contradiction, then, is neither structural nor technical; it is tonal. Of the terms suggested above only irony applies. One major facet of that irony is directed at Gawain himself, since he alone accepts the value the lady puts on the silk sash. He accepts the magic, of course, because he wants to, and he accepts the gift because he "cares for his life." He carefully girds himself with it when he goes to meet his fate, but apparently does not think about it again until the denouement and Bercilak's explanations. Then he adopts it as an ironic symbol of his fault, and upon his return to Camelot the entire court adopts it in such a way as to invert the irony again, to lighten it, and to turn it again in the direction of Gawain in tones which are affectionate, urbane, and humane— not the penitential anguish he has affected himself.

The point of beginning with these observations is, first, that *Gawain* criticism everywhere talks about a magic girdle without ever remarking that it is not magic at all. It cannot and does not protect Gawain. (Apply this point to the rest of the poem, and what happens to the lame dependence on Morgan, which, too, has been taken incredibly seriously?) Second, *Gawain* criticism, though sometimes—especially recently—paying lip service to the poem's comedic tones, is usually pretentiously serious and portentously heavyhanded. And third, Raffel's translation has so accurately caught the tone—that use of romance material for an urbane and humane irony not without gentle satire, that good-humored narrative style which can and does handle serious matters with sophisticated wit and wisdom— that one must affirm the absolute rightness of it.

Since the following comments on *Gawain* include comments on the *Gawain* scholarship as well, at the outset I should acknowledge that my greatest debts are to Larry D. Benson, whose *Art and Tradition in Sir Gawain and the Green Knight* is the most illuminating single treatment of the poem (Benson has located the poem in the context of literary history: the following remarks are at best only sketchy suggestions by comparison—a service station roadmap to his Baedeker); to Marie Borroff, whose *Sir Gawain and the Green Knight: A Stylistic and Metrical Study* is very important to any attempt to discuss the metrics of the poem; and to *Critical Studies of Sir Gawain and the Green Knight,* edited by Donald R. Howard and Christian Zacher (Notre Dame, 1968, part of Notre Dame's excellent series of critical studies), the best of the collections of essays on the poem, judicious in its choice, and having the good judgment to begin with Morton Bloomfield's distinguished essay "*Sir Gawain and the Green Knight:* An Appraisal," with which anyone's study of the scholarship on the poem might well begin.

It is safe to say that *Gawain* is one of the most nearly unanimously admired pieces of literature in western culture. Scholars and critics express their uniformly high regard for it while they devote their professional attention to it. And the activities of the editors and translators provide ample additional testimony to that admiration and regard. Yet surely part of the appeal of *Gawain* for these very special audiences lies in the very problems and mysteries attached to it or associated with it.

Not the least of these attractions is its use of Arthurian romance material. Anything connected with this massive cycle, which has become an agglomeration of multiple and diverse elements out of a variety of cultures and traditions, has the magnetic appeal of the whole subject, partaking of the sacred mysteries of Arthurian sources, developments, and semiology. And the relationship of *Gawain* to Arthurian material is not the least of the problems in a study of the poem. The general view at this time seems to be that the poem is directly in the mainstream of Arthurian transmission, traceable back through the French tradition to the Celtic, probably by way of Breton, and with some potential backwash from the German tributary.

Perhaps the most magnetic of these *Gawain* mysteries is the fact that the poem, so patently sophisticated and original as it is, is also demonstrably conventional and traditional. In the absence of extant evidence of a long-flourishing tradition standing behind the poem, one can only react with wonderment and awe. Reason, or perhaps it is only rationalization, tells us that such a tradition must have existed, that it must have a direct connection with the rich Old English poetic tradition, and that the *Gawain*-poet—though a genius—could not have operated in a cultural vacuum. *Gawain,* after all, shows evidence not only of a broadly based appeal to the material of traditional romance (as well as *fabliau,* drama, folk tale, and perhaps heroic epic) but also of a broadly based familiarity with the high-cultural traditions of nearly contemporary Europe. Benson gives a rewarding and full account of these appeals.

We call him the *Gawain*-poet simply because we do not know his identity. Attempts to name names, a fascinating but generally unproductive activity of literary detectives, began with Sir Frederic Madden's 1839 edition for the Bannatyne Club, which suggests Huchown of the Awle Ryle and Ralph Strode as possibilities, and have continued to the present with such nominees as John Donne, John Prat, John Erghome, and Hugh Mascy. The most detailed case has been made out by Henry L. Savage, *The Gawain-Poet: Studies in His Personality and Background* (Chapel Hill, 1956). Very tentatively, and with a charmingly old-fashioned style, Savage connects the poem with a large number of historical events in and around the life of Enguerrand, Sire de Coucy. For a critical approach to the poem, however, Savage's major contribution appears in his second chapter, which contains excellent explication of the allegory, symbolism, and structure of the hunting/castle scenes.

Related to the problem of the poet's identity is the question of whether the same man is responsible for *Pearl, Purity,* and *Patience,* the three other poems which appear with *Gawain* in the unique manuscript, Cotton Nero A x. One other poem, *St. Erkenwald,* is often assigned to him too, but Benson has convincingly dismissed it from the "canon." The overwhelmingly prevalent opinion is that one artist composed all four poems, but the matter is by no means proved. I expect that when viable computer programs are set up for the study of stylistics, more evidence will be produced. But this will not be proof either: traditional styles by their very nature often defy positive assignments of common authorship.

There is similar general agreement on the matters of provenance and dialect, with perhaps some weightier evidence and more disciplined inferences—but not proved. It seems to me that, without much qualitative loss to the study of the poem, these questions of identity, canon, and dialect can be set aside with the very general assignment of provenance to the late fourteenth century in the Northwest Midlands. This is the time and the place often pointed to as the center of the Alliterative Revival, that sudden outburst of stored-up domestic poetic energies which hearkened back to a tradition that had been virtually silent since 991.

That tradition, itself based on a poetics of traditional oral style, had left practically no manuscript records for almost four centuries. But it is important to remember that there was precious little English poetry of any kind recorded during those centuries. The whole language went underground beneath the twin tyrannies of church and state, so that Latin and French were the officially acceptable and *publishable* languages. The second half of the fourteenth century, then, saw the revival of English as the official language and a publishable one, and the traditional alliterative verse which had been going on and developing along several lines became visible again. And it stands to reason that the underground would be strongest in direct ratio to distance from the capitals. Thus, whether the distance was that of class, attitude, culture, or simply geography, the various demonstrations of "alliterative survival" can be accounted for.

In his Preface, Raffel speaks of the complexity and brilliance of the poem, especially its *exterior*. Yet the scholarly admiration for *Gawain* has often been transformed into energy spent on seeking the key to its meaning, looking at the *interior* to discover the single theme that informs and controls all that brilliance and complexity. On the face of it, such an approach would seem to be doomed to failure, and the results bear out the appearance. Theme-naming, by taking you inside the poem, will take you away from it.

Perhaps this is what Benson means when he says that "the subject of this romance is romance itself." Yet even Benson is drawn on, in the only flawed part of his book, to discuss the theme of the poem as *renown*. Burrow, on the other hand, sees the theme as "*truth,* in the medieval sense of the word." Burrow's *Reading* is a pretty pedestrian one, but he must be given credit for attempting to explore the orthodox Christianity of the poem and put it into perspective, as part of its "comic version of Everyman":

> To some extent the poet presents the cycle of experience in terms of the appropriate Christian ritual—the ritual of Penance—just as he projects it in terms of the appropriate Christian myth—the myth of Judgment./. . . Dogmas do not matter here: Bercilak can be God, priest, man and super-ego, all at once and without inconsistency. What does matter is the fundamental cycle of experience, and this must in the last analysis be stated quite abstractly, however bald the statement may sound—as a cycle of social living, alienation, self-discovery, desolation, recovery and restoration. This, or something like it, is the abstract comic form of the poem.
>
> *(J. A. Burrow,* A Reading of Sir Gawain and the Green Knight, *p. 186)*

Unfortunately, Burrow comes to terms with penance far more comfortably than he comes to terms with comedy.

The need for perspective with regard to the Christian elements is especially apparent under the pervasive influence of D. W. Robertson. What purports to be a historical approach is actually a practice of searching out patristic authority for the superimposition of a moralistic Christian preachment upon any medieval text. Thus Hans Schnyder (*Sir Gawain and the Green Knight,* Bern, 1961) says that "it is only in the historical perspective of medieval allegory that *Sir Gawain and the Green Knight* can be interpreted as a unity of inner plausibility and coherence." (P. 74) His analysis is broken down in sections called "The Fabulous Narrative," "The Proud King," "The Anxious Journey," "The Three Temptations," and "The Descent." This terminology is so transparent that it needs no comment. But what about the poem, the quality of its poetry? Well, "conventional allegorical concepts" have been infused "with real life" to achieve "the highest type of allegory—a type that was even in the Middle Ages the exception rather than the norm—where the artistic appreciation of material things combines harmoniously with their allegorical meaning." (P. 74)

Richard Hamilton Green makes some use of the scholarly apparatus of patristics, along with allegory and iconography, but his generalizations about the poem indicate that he feels the emphasis should be placed elsewhere ("Gawain's Shield and the Quest for Perfection," in Blanch). M. Mills, too, has tried to give Schnyder's view an appropriately small place: allegory no, suggestions yes; just as *Gawain*'s audience would have responded to "old Gawain" suggestions from romance tradition, so they must have picked up Christian exegetical material *in potentia* ("Christian Significance and Romance Tradition in *Sir Gawain and the Green Knight,*" in Howard-Zacher). Jan Solomon sees "The Lesson of Sir Gawain" as an allegorical demonstration of the value of *mesure,* humility, or moderation as opposed to the evils of pride, *desmesure,* and *surfet* (Howard-Zacher); and David Farley Hills places the theme in the Augustinian tradition of *cupiditas* ("Gawain's Fault in *Sir Gawain and the Green Knight,*" Howard-Zacher, followed by Burrow's sensible reply). But the Robertsonian doctrine is carried furthest along by Bernard S. Levy, "Gawain's Spiritual Journey: *Imitatio Christi* in *Sir Gawain and the Green Knight*" (*Annuale Mediaevale,* VI [1966], 65–106). A playful antidote to the patristic approach should have been found in Stephen Manning, "A Psychological Interpretation of *Sir Gawain and the Green Knight*" (Howard-Zacher), which gives the poem a Jungian reading: "The ego's encounter with the shadow." Unfortunately, the premise, which elicits such high hopes for a clever *jeu d'esprit,* is not carried out. Manning's wit fails as he gets carried away with his idea. He takes it seriously, carries it through laboriously, and by the end has convinced himself—if no one else.

We may agree with Bloomfield that "the poem is fairly and squarely Christian," which is really no more than to say that its Christian material is not a product of monkish interpolation. Of course not, but that doesn't mean that it must be allegorical. Perhaps *here* is where the lesson of moderation applies: any attempt to reduce a poem like this to a single message/statement/theme/principle/source/meaning is doomed to failure, however gracious the style of the attempt.

But the Robertsonian heresy is not the only process of *reductio ad absurdum* that has attacked *Gawain.* Despite C. S. Lewis's and Kittredge's warnings about mare's nests and pan-Celtic Cloudcuckooland, the ritual and myth critics have had at the poem with a vengeance. Even two distinguished orientalists, Heinrich Zimmer (in *The King and the Corpse,* New York, 1956) and Ananda K. Coomaraswamy ("Sir Gawain and the Green Knight: Indra and Namuci," *Speculum,* XIX [1944], 104–125) have seen in it examples of an archetypal voyage to the underworld which is a type of sacrificial death and rebirth. Coomaraswamy also finds parallels, for other motifs in the poem, in ancient Indian sources as well as in Amerindian legend. A. H. Krappe should also be noted here for his similar folkloristic approach ("Who *Was* the Green Knight?" *Speculum,* XIII [1938], 206–215).

The idea of *Gawain* as a vegetation myth was suggested somewhat obliquely by William A. Nitze in 1936 ("Is the Green Knight a Vegetation Myth?" *Modern Philology,* XXXVII, 351–366), and carried through by John Speirs (in Fox). But Charles Moorman, strenuously objecting to misuse of the myth-ritual approach (especially by Zimmer and Speirs), goes on to apply a *rites de passage* pattern to the poem, with some rather distorting results (in Blanch). It may be worth noting here that Speirs's reading begins with the *metaphor* of the poem's organic unity and then projects that metaphor into a systematic explication of a "seasonal theme . . . the poem's underlying, indeed pervasive theme." (Fox, p. 83)

The unpublished dissertation of Sally P. Kennedy (Univ. of Tennessee, 1968) takes a new direction toward ultimate source-material and therefore underlying meanings. Most of all, it is an attempt to account for universal appeal. She uses a ritual-mythic approach, too, but unlike the pervasive vegetation, fertility, and initiation theories, she examines the poem in the context of rule ritual, specifically in terms of a prehistoric matriarchal-patriarchal conflict which came to be celebrated in many familiar ritual and narrative motifs. In this context, a new angle of approach is made toward many elements in the poem: the calendar of events, the contrasting settings, the roles of the ladies at Bercilak's castle, the green chapel, Gawain as king's sister's son and as surrogate for Arthur, the beheading game, the green girdle, the nick on the neck, the clothing and arming of Gawain, and certain aspects of the hunt. Miss Kennedy's investigation parallels my own line of investigation, a tentative statement of which is found in "Royal Robes and Regicide," *Folk-*

lore, LXXX (1969), 191–215. Part of our working hypothesis was anticipated, in a super-Freudian framework, by Géza Róheim in 1930 (*Animism, Magic, and The Divine King,* pp. 289–297), which so far as I know has never appeared in any *Gawain* bibliography.

But source-studies do not always deal with ultimates. The business of constructing genealogies often places more emphasis on immediate ancestors. It is sometimes difficult to separate out the sources from the analogues; but in any case, the formidable names of J. R. Hulbert, George Lyman Kittredge, and Jessie L. Weston may be consulted for accounts of Irish, Welsh, French, and German parallels: Hulbert, "Syr Gawayne and the Grene Knyʒt," *Modern Philology,* XIII (1916), 433–462, 689–730; Kittredge, *A Study of Sir Gawain and the Green Knight* (Cambridge, Mass., 1916); Weston, *The Legend of Sir Gawain* (London, 1897) and *From Ritual to Romance* (Cambridge, England, 1920).

For example, a study underway at present by Alice Lasater at the University of Tennessee seeks to establish the meaning of observed relationships between the work of the *Gawain*-poet and Hispano-Arabic traditions. Miss Lasater notes that "A particularly close parallel exists . . . between the green knight and a benevolent green figure in Arabic lore, known through the *Hadiths* and appearing in several tales of the *Arabian Nights.* The 'green one' represents divine law and justice, often requires a quest and testing of the hero, and often initiates a challenge when he appears in a court. Whatever his Celtic ancestry, the green knight also shows kinship to the Arabic figure and may well be a descendant of both." Moreover, she suspects that there may be other connections, including a relationship between the literary courtly love tradition and *The Dove's Neckring* by Ibn Hazm, written in Aragon in the eleventh century, and the possibility that the *Gawain*-poet's prosody was influenced by Spanish-Arabic troubador art, perhaps by way of French troubadors and *trouvères.*

Scholarly admiration for *Gawain* has been evidenced in other ways, too, and it would be well to note the contributions of the philologists. "Philology," Bloomfield says, "must remain the basis of all sound literary work or we shall end in a morass of subjectivism." He goes on to say that of the three main philological activities, the first, the establishment of a text, has been virtually completed, barring the discovery of a new manuscript of *Gawain*. The second and third, identification of dialect and determination of the meaning of words, go on with the promise of new assistance from the *English Dialect Dictionary,* from the *Middle English Dictionary,* from the completed study of English place names, and from a linguistic atlas of England. Bloomfield also urges a combination of literary sensitivity, common sense, and philology—a combination, incidentally, which would be especially attractive in a future edition of the poem. I have found, like Raffel, that the TGD is the handiest edition to use, but it should not be relied on exclusively. Always consult the edition of Gollancz, Day, and Serjeantson (EETS, 1940) for alternate readings and especially for differing explanations in the notes.

In recent years, however, critical appreciation for *Gawain* has mainly produced energy for studies of its art, resulting in many attempts to probe what Raffel has called its exceedingly brilliant and complex exterior. Of the twenty-three items in Howard-Zacher, no fewer than eleven are examples of these attempts, examining elements of style, structure, and technique and particularities of images, characters, and settings. As examples of constructive and illuminating contributions along these lines, one may profitably consider three essays by Alain Renoir. The first ("Descriptive Techniques in Sir Gawain and the Green Knight," *Orbis Litterarum,* XIII [1958], 126–132) suggests that the poet's descriptive technique is basically analogous with motion picture technique. The second ("The Progressive Magnification: an Instance of Psychological Description in *Sir Gawain and the Green Knight,*"

Moderna Sprak, LIV [1960], 245–253) shows the relationship between visual descriptions and Gawain's states of mind. The third (in Howard-Zacher) demonstrates the importance of *sound,* patterns of aural imagery supporting the more obvious visual impressions.

I have talked about scholarly *admiration* for *Gawain* and critical *appreciation* of its art, but what has too infrequently been acknowledged is that the admiration and the appreciation are exceeded only by *affection* for the poem. Artistry of technique, integration of materials, and projections of levels of meaning may account for the admiration, but only tone can account for the affection. In fact, at the risk of making the monolithic mistake I have found in other critics, I would assert that its tone so thoroughly informs the processes of *Gawain* and governs responses to the poem that no statement of its meaning or art makes complete sense outside its tonal context. As the integrating technique of the whole poem, its tone leads to the discovery of its meaning; or, baldly to assert Mark Schorer's principle, the tone is the meaning.

Raffel agrees with Benson that *Gawain* is "predominantly a festive poem," and Benson concludes, "English literature may offer a few, very few better narratives than *Sir Gawain and the Green Knight,* but none more delightful and humane." Many others, while discussing rather more serious aspects, have commended its comedy, its irony, its wit, its good nature, and its fun. Green: "pervasive comic irony" (in Blanch); Bloomfield: "at the same time witty, ironical, and religious" (in Howard-Zacher), and he mentions Elizabeth M. Wright, G. H. Gerould, and John Conley as professing a similar view; Howard: "spirit of amused and ironic detachment" (in Howard-Zacher and in Fox); Sacvan Bercovitch: "overriding comic-realistic spirit which good-naturedly laughs" (Howard-Zacher); E. Talbot Donaldson: "a rare combination: at once a comedy—even a satire—of manners and a profoundly Christian view of man's character and his destiny" (in Fox); and Burrow: "a *comic* poem—by which I mean not so much a poem full of fun and games (though it is that), as a poem which ends happily with the hero reincorporated into his society" (*Reading,* p. 185).

The nearest approach to a full treatment of the festive tone is that of R. H. Bowers, "*Gawain and the Green Knight* as Entertainment" (in Howard-Zacher). Bowers says, "The high comedy of *Sir Gawain and the Green Knight* is accentuated by the constant laughter that occurs throughout the poem. I do not believe that the laughter and gay spirit of the poem has been sufficiently emphasized. . . . I read the laughter . . . as good-natured and gay." And again, ". . . the laughter in *Sir Gawain and the Green Knight* should be granted its proper place in setting the tone and hence the meaning of the poem. The poet sees the idea of chivalry whole, with affection and good-natured understanding. . . ." He also refers to the "over-all context of practical joking" within which the two confessions should not be taken as seriously as they have been by Burrow and others. Curiously enough, though Bowers begins by saying that the "aspect of delight and entertainment . . . is in danger of being submerged by too much solemn, somber criticism," he spends most of his time seriously disputing other readings, especially those of Markham, Moorman, and Burrow.

The alliterative metric of *Gawain* looks back to the native tradition of Old English poetry. As it appears in *Beowulf,* composed in a traditional, oral style, the verse is arranged (according to the influential reconstruction of John Collins Pope in *The Rhythm of Beowulf*) in roughly isochronous measures accompanied by a regular harp beat—one per measure, falling on the accented syllable but occasionally on initial rests. The line consists of four measures, actually two half-lines (verses) of two measures each, and these verses are linked together (*soðe gebunden* "truly bound" *Beowulf* 871a) by alliteration or initial rhyme. The whole line, then, is the basic unit, and the *scops* composed by building lines from a store of rhythmic-semantic-syntactic patterns called formulas arranged in alliterating pairs. The alliteration that counts is what holds the lines together, and the alliterating syllable in each verse occupies the primary stress. It is the *pair* of alliterating syllables around which the rest of the line forms. Other alliterations, when they occur, do not influence or alter the natural and necessary rhythmic structure. They are incidental or accidental.

Naturally, in a poetic form geared to the effects of alliteration, the effects will be cultivated and the alliterations will proliferate. But before suggesting how this cultivation and proliferation contributed to the fourteenth-century alliterative form, I would make a few other fairly basic observations about the Old English form. First, syllable length may be discounted in rhythmic analysis because there is no *necessary* correlation between stress and time. Unlike classical Latin meters, Old English poetry determines stress by alliteration, natural accent, rhetorical emphasis, and syntactical priority (in that order), and not by length (whether physiological, etymological, or positional).

Second, an essential part of the rhythm is syncopation—the displacement of regular rhythmic beat so that one syllable (or note) crosses the imaginary bar-division between measures and shares some of the time of both measures. For example, a regular form of | bum diddy | bum diddy | may be syncopated to | bum di bum | m diddy | . A sustained rhythmic performance or sustained isochrony is difficult to conceive of without syncopation, but nearly impossible in a musically accompanied form. The use of a small harp or lyre in the poetry is not merely the hypothesis of Pope's brilliant account; it is attested to by frequent references in the poetry itself and proved by fragments of a small stringed instrument unearthed at Sutton Hoo.

The basic verse patterns achieve a pleasant variety-in-regularity both by the shifting arrangement of the accented syllables and by the constantly changing number and placement of unaccented syllables. And finally, the basic verse is sometimes attenuated, either with an interjectory syllable *(Hwæt)* which stands outside the pattern and probably should receive an extra harp stroke or with a full "expanded verse" of three measures (n.b.: it is often difficult to distinguish expanded verses from crowded regular verses, particularly where incidental alliteration occurs).

Whether or not *Beowulf,* as we know it, was orally composed, the fact is that by the end of the tenth century, in *The Battle of Maldon*—a poem *written* in the traditional oral style—a number of developments and trends may be seen in the metrics. *Maldon* remains heavily formulaic, the basic alliterative patterns are maintained, and the nearly absolute integrity of the half-lines (rhythmic, semantic, and syntactic) is sustained. But the average number of unaccented syllables is larger, the arrangement of these unaccented syllables is more casual, the number of incidental and secondary alliterations increases, and the lines become far more regularly end-stopped. Add to these developments the following three centuries of French domination/contact/contamination in language and culture, and you have the background for the Middle English forms of alliteration.

In *Piers Plowman* the distance from *Maldon* is more obvious than it is in *Gawain.* Langland's verse is formulaic, but the formulas give the impression of stale tags and alliterative clichés. Their effect matches that of the poem itself, an automatic appeal to popular taste out of the storehouse of common experience. Alliteration remains, and the pattern has expanded to include a second regular alliteration in the first half-line, with much additional secondary alliteration. The lines are infallibly end-stopped, but the semantic and syntactic integrity of the half-lines has been enforced at the expense of rhythmic integrity. Thus, the rough-and-ready quality of many of the crowded on-verses belies the rigidity of the composition. Though Langland often employs Latin, without breaking his rhythmic patterns, his verse displays none of the familiar influences of Romance prosody—syllable counting, pseudo-quantity, rhyme, "foreign" diction. The attempt to abjure an artistic style seems quite deliberate, but this is perhaps the virtue and the achievement of Langland's broad employment of conventions of allegory, dream vision, and popular drama.

Turning to *Gawain,* we find a more consciously artistic blending of the traditional forms and new conventions of high style. We also find, it seems to me, an admirable blend of native and continental cultures, not just in subject-matter but in formal elements as well. Marie Borroff, whose book begins with an admirable, elaborate attempt to provide a theoretical framework for the criticism of style, is worth quoting at length in this regard:

The language of *Sir Gawain and the Green Knight* is thoroughly traditional. Where he is original, the poet may rather be said to add to the tradition than to depart from it. The store of stock phrases, of set patterns, of ways of building the line, of modes of reference, of qualitative adjectives, which was drawn on by the *Gawain*-poet, was drawn on equally by the other poets. These characteristic features of style are historically determined: the *Gawain*-poet was born into the tradition in which he wrote. But from the point of view of the criticism of style, features become devices. The superiority of *Gawain* over other poems belonging to the same tradition consists not in the devices themselves but in what they accomplish. In the hands of the mediocre poet the technical resources of the alliterative style merely make possible the construction of the line. In the hands of the *Gawain*-poet these resources take on poetic power: the technical problems of the line are not merely solved but transcended. The result is "þe best boke of romaunce." *(p. 90)*

Following her detailed discussions, we can make a number of generalizations about the metrics of *Gawain*. The line has a four-stress basis: no other system works for so many lines. The crowded lines containing five chief syllables (three, with at least two alliterating, in the on-verse) may often be read as four-stress, with one of the alliterating syllables in the on-verse recognized as subordinate (Borroff's "supernumerary," my "incidental" alliteration). This is particularly convenient where there is extra alliteration on prepositions and unaccented prefixes. The alliterative line is closer to the spoken language than rhymed forms, because accentuation is more natural and flexible. Yet there is a tendency toward isochrony (more apparent in *Gawain* than in *Piers*) which separates metrical rhythms from prose or ordinary speech. *Piers* may be performed as a kind of rhythmic preachment/declamation/drama; *Gawain* may be recited as a kind of *a cappella* concert-piece.

Benson has pointed out that some of the changes in the alliterative style must have been determined by the changes in the language itself as well as changes in "the conditions of composition and performance." (P. 114) But others are surely due to the cross-fertilization of cultures. Thus, whereas in *Piers* the infallible end-stopping is accompanied by a rigidity of half-line units, in *Gawain* the regularly end-stopped lines are accompanied by a subtle underplaying of the half-line divisions. The divisions are still there—and I believe that several cruces in the poem can be resolved by applying a principle of half-line integrity—but they are less noticeable. Indeed, where no clear caesura can be established, the lack is not disconcerting.

The bob-and-wheel pattern which ends every strophe is the clearest demonstration of the poet's triumphal integration of formal materials. These sections are rhymed, syllabically regular, accentually precise, rhythmically sustained, and heavily alliterative. And they work. To quote Marie Borroff again, ". . . meter is stylistically effective—effective not in itself but in relation to the content and detail of the narrative, the meanings expressed, and the kinds of words used to express them. . . . The sounds and rhythms of words are essential to the style of *Sir Gawain and the Green Knight.*" (P. 210) I would add that Raffel's handling of these aspects of form is a triumph in itself.

Burton Raffel's translation of *Gawain* is brilliant. It is the translation the poem deserves. He has avoided the pitfalls that have trapped earlier attempts: too slavish emulation of the metrics (particularly difficult where technical and formal aspects of the verse were only dimly perceived); too slavish imitation of the diction (the effect of the sophisticated high style is destroyed by precious archaizing); and too slavish attention to a word-by-word literalness in translation (this can only lead to prose, with a loss that goes far beyond metrical matters to do damage to the *sense* that comes with form, style, and tone).

Where useful, Raffel has borrowed the poet's own rhetorical devices, such as his unobtrusive use of many conjunctions (the classical figure *polysyndeton*) where pacing needs to be sustained. Sometimes he has actually improved on the poet's device, such as making the bob an essential part of the preceding line (cf. Raffel's integration with the *Gawain*-poet's at lines 385, 486, 531, 635, 665, 686, etc.). Actually, in the manuscript, the bob is written—after a gap—at the end of the last long line of a strophe. One is tempted to say that this is a graphic equivalent of the effect in recitation. The extra beat in the long line signals the approaching end of a passage and at the same time initiates the graceful pattern that closes or encloses or summarizes a segment. Sometimes, choruslike, the wheel may look beyond, and here too the bob is a vital signal for attention. Raffel's free half-rhyming in the bob-and-wheel solves the problems presented by the form far better than any other translation I know of.

Sometimes, by a subtle rearrangement of parts, Raffel has achieved an effect which may have been intended for the original audience but has been lost in the six intervening centuries. A simple example is his "courteously, but loud" at line 469, which so plainly captures Arthur's frame of mind and the poet's point. Where there is unmeaningful ambiguity in the text, as in line 1884—*As domez day schulde haf ben di3t on þe morn*—Raffel can deftly supply the single meaning which seems to be called for: "the Day/Of Judgment could have come with the sun, and been welcome." And where formulaic language echoes within the poem, this translator's ear picks it up and transplants it without drawing attention to the process (for example, lines 1478 and 1981). Finally, there are times when he can bring new illumination to the text, as in the scene where Arthur orders the axe hung as a trophy (lines 476 ff.): for the first time I was shown the possibility of an ironic reference to the corresponding, traditional detail in *Beowulf*.

For, as Robert P. Creed has said in his foreword to *Poems from the Old English,* Raffel is a poet. In "tracking" the poem (the term is Raffel's own) he has recaptured it. He "solves" cruces by not allowing them to interrupt the workings of his sure poetic instinct, and his diction and rhythms have produced an exciting equivalent to this fourteenth-century masterpiece. Best of all, he has reproduced the festive, comic, ironic, sophisticated, urbane, and humane tone of the original.

—Neil D. Isaacs
February, 1970
Knoxville, Tennessee

SELECTED BIBLIOGRAPHY

Several books cited only in the Afterword
are here included; however, in all cases
the annotations are by the translator.

Benson, Larry D., *Art and Tradition in Sir Gawain
and the Green Knight*, Rutgers University Press,
1965. Sensitive *and* learned discussion of sources;
literary convention and characterization; style;
narrative and descriptive techniques; meaning.
The book is modest in tone but richly informative;
much the best study in print.

Blanch, Robert J., ed., *Sir Gawain and Pearl: Critical
Essays*, Indiana U.P., 1966. Very much a mixed
bag: six essays, some of them horrendously awful,
some spottily intelligent. Not recommended.

Borroff, Marie, *Sir Gawain and the Green Knight: A
Stylistic and Metrical Study*, Yale U.P., 1962. A
rather ponderous, wordy, and frequently insensi-
tive study of difficult matters; sometimes useful,
but to be consulted with caution, despite the
heavy scholarly apparatus.

Burrow, J. A., *A Reading of Sir Gawain and the Green
Knight*, Routledge & Kegan Paul, 1965. Literary
criticism on a very low level, though sometimes
dully effective. Not recommended.

Fox, Denton, ed., *Twentieth Century Interpretations of
Sir Gawain and The Green Knight*, Prentice–Hall,
1968. A brief but sometimes rewarding collection;

some of the essays are at best spottily intelligent, but the selection is distinctly superior to that in the Blanch compendium. Recommended, with due caution.

Howard, Donald R. and Christian Zacher, eds., *Critical Studies of Sir Gawain and the Green Knight*, University of Notre Dame Press, 1968. Useful; fuller than the Fox collection; sometimes a bit pedantic.

Kittredge, George Lyman, *A Study of Gawain and the Green Knight*, Peter Smith, 1960 (first printed in 1916). A highly speculative, well-written study devoted exclusively to literary sources, actual, possible, and imaginary. Of moderate interest, if used both sparingly and appropriately.

Longnon, Jean, and Raymond Cazelles, eds., *The Très Riches Heures of Jean, Duke of Berry*, George Braziller, 1969. No direct connection with *Sir Gawain and the Green Knight*, but many of the illustrations—beautifully reproduced—are vivid evocations of the spirit, and often much of the detail, of the poem.

Loomis, Roger Sherman, *The Development of Arthurian Romances*, Harper Torchbooks, 1964. Biased and crotchety, but clear and, for the beginner, modestly informative; deeply traditional, hostile to much in contemporary criticism. Recommended, if used with due caution.

Savage, Henry L., *The Gawain–Poet: Studies in His Personality and Background*, University of North Carolina Press, 1956. A set of crotchety historical essays having no proven connection to the Gawain-poet and no relevance whatever to the poem. Not recommended.

CLASSIC TALES OF MEDIEVAL CHIVALRY

IDYLLS OF THE KING & Selected Poems
Alfred Lord Tennyson
Tennyson's dramatic retelling of the Legend of Arthur and his knights in poetic form. Both delightful and dramatic, this is Tennyson's masterpiece.

LE MORTE D'ARTHUR
Sir Thomas Malory
Sir Thomas Malory gathered together a number of disparate tales of Arthur and his Round Table and made them into one long work which is an exciting and entertaining tale. First printed in 1485, it has become the basis for most of the Arthurian narratives written since.

Available wherever books are sold or at
signetclassics.com

S400

The Great Epic Poems

BEOWULF
translated by Burton Raffel
This poem, one of the earliest poems in English, is the story of a young and adventurous knight who comes to the aid of an elderly king. Through his acts of bravery, Beowulf proves himself worthy of a kingdom of his own.

THE ILIAD
translated by W.H.D. Rouse
This very readable prose translation tells the tale of Achilles, Hector, Agamemnon, Paris, Helen, and all of Troy besieged by the mighty Greeks. It is a tale of glory and honor, of pride and pettiness, of friendship and sacrifice, of anger and revenge. In short, it is the quintessential western tale of men at war.

THE ODYSSEY
translated by W.H.D. Rouse
Kept away from his home and family for 20 years by war and malevolent gods, Odysseus returns to find his house in disarray. This is the story of his adventurous travels and his battle to reclaim what is rightfully his.

THE CANTERBURY TALES: A Selection
Geoffrey Chaucer
This unique edition maintains much of the middle English text, while at the same time incorporating normalized contemporary spellings to produce a text that is both easy to read and faithful to the sound and sense of Chaucer's original. This volume contains all of the most famous tales, from the mirthful to the bawdy to the profoundly moral, reflecting not only the manners and mores of medieval England, but indeed the full comic and tragic dimensions of life.

EPIC TALES

THE THREE MUSKETEERS
by Alexandre Dumas

The Three Musketeers is the most famous of Alexandre Dumas's historical novels and one of the most popular adventure stories ever written. This swashbuckling epic chronicles the adventures of d'Artagnan, a brash young man from the countryside who journeys to Paris in 1625 hoping to become a musketeer and guard to King Louis XIII. Before long he finds treachery and court intrigue—and also three boon companions: the daring swordsmen Athos, Porthos, and Aramis. Together they strive heroically to defend the honor of their queen against the powerful Cardinal Richelieu and the seductive spy Milady.

DON QUIXOTE: Complete and Unabridged
by Miguel de Cervantes

This is the epic tale of Don Quixote de La Mancha and his faithful squire, Sancho Panza. Their picaresque adventures in the world of sixteenth-century Spain form the basis of one of the great treasures of Western literature—a book that is both an immortal satire on an outdated chivalric code and a biting portrayal of an age in which nobility can be a form of madness. Imbued with superb comedy and irony, *Don Quixote* stands as a testament to the author's rich artistry.

READ THE TOP 20
SIGNET CLASSICS

ANIMAL FARM BY GEORGE ORWELL

1984 BY GEORGE ORWELL

THE INFERNO BY DANTE

FRANKENSTEIN BY MARY SHELLEY

BEOWULF (BURTON RAFFEL, TRANSLATOR)

THE ODYSSEY BY HOMER

THE FEDERALIST PAPERS BY ALEXANDER HAMILTON

THE HOUND OF THE BASKERVILLES
    BY SIR ARTHUR CONAN DOYLE

NARRATIVE OF THE LIFE OF FREDERICK DOUGLASS
    BY FREDERICK DOUGLASS

DR. JEKYLL AND MR. HYDE BY ROBERT LOUIS STEVENSON

HAMLET BY WILLIAM SHAKESPEARE

THE SCARLET LETTER BY NATHANIEL HAWTHORNE

LES MISÉRABLES BY VICTOR HUGO

HEART OF DARKNESS AND THE SECRET SHARER
    BY JOSEPH CONRAD

WUTHERING HEIGHTS BY EMILY BRONTË

A MIDSUMMER NIGHT'S DREAM BY WILLIAM SHAKESPEARE

NECTAR IN A SIEVE BY KAMALA MARKANDAYA

ETHAN FROME BY EDITH WHARTON

ADVENTURES OF HUCKLEBERRY FINN BY MARK TWAIN

A TALE OF TWO CITIES BY CHARLES DICKENS

SIGNETCLASSICS.COM
FACEBOOK.COM/SIGNETCLASSIC